AN ESSENTIAL

CHINA'S POPULAR
DESTINATIONS

CW00429475

Better Link Press

Copyright © 2010 Shanghai Press and Publishing Development Company

This book is edited and designed by the Editorial Committee of *Cultural China* series

Managing Directors: Wang Youbu, Xu Naiqing
Editorial Director: Wu Ying
Editors: Ye Jiasheng, Anna Nguyen
Editorial Assistant: Li Mengyao

Text by Dong Huai
Images by Quanjing, Phototime, 8danyuan
Cover Image: Getty Images

Cover Design: Wang Wei
Interior Design: Yuan Yinchang, Li Jing, Xia Wei

ISBN: 978-1-60220-602-1

Address any comments about *An Essential Guide to China's Popular Destinations* to:

Better Link Press
99 Park Ave
New York, NY 10016
USA
or
Shanghai Press and Publishing Development Company
F 7 Donghu Road, Shanghai, China (200031)
Email: comments_betterlinkpress@hotmail.com

Printed in China by Shanghai Donnelley Printing Co. Ltd.

1 2 3 4 5 6 7 8 9 10

Contents

Contents

Stop 5: Guilin ··········103

Get Started Here

Stop 6: Hong Kong ········113

Get Started Here

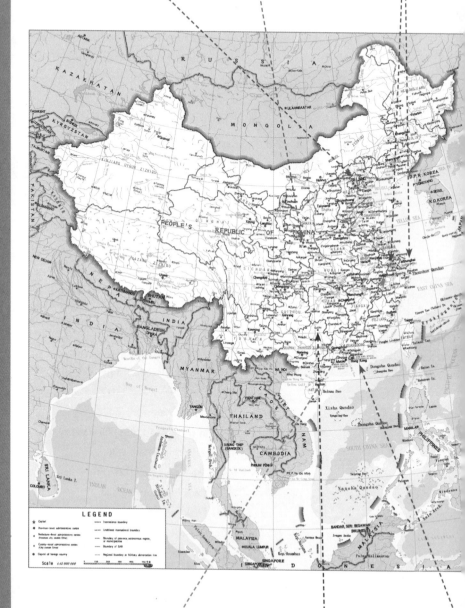

Preface

If you have only ten days to spend in China, what places should you not miss? Although it is impossible to travel all around this large territory in a few days, you can still go to some representative cities to experience China's unique landscape, culture, history, and the dynamic rhythm of its development.

The seven places recommended in this book scatter in different regions of China. They possess distinguished features and praise from tourist for beauty achieved both by nature and historical changes spanning over thousand years. Immerse yourself in China's rich history in imperial Beijing and its ancient capital of Xi'an. In contrast, take in the energetic and progressive cities of Hong Kong and Shanghai to experience modern China. To take a break from the action, relax in the picturesque settings of Suzhou and Hangzhou, Which have both been called "heaven on earth." In Guilin, you'll find breathtaking landscapes praised as the best in country.

As Shanghai and Suzhou are adjacent to each other, they are arranged together in one stop. Each section contains highlights meant to suit a variety of interests. Visitors will find cultural and historic sights, shopping and entertainment, and spectacular city and natural landscapes while traveling in China. This journey of six coherent, but distinctive stops will show you the diversified beauty of China.

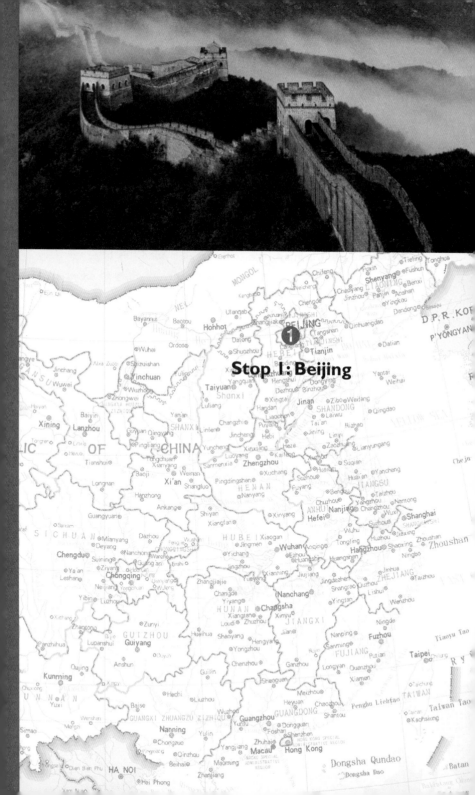

Stop I: Beijing

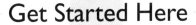

Get Started Here

General Information

Beijing, also called Jing for short, is the capital of the People's Republic of China. It is a municipality directly under the central government that is opening up to the outside world. With 16 districts and 2 counties under its administrative jurisdiction, Beijing has a total area of 16,800 sq. km and a population of 16 million, with the ethnic groups of the Han, Man, Hui, and Mongol.

Environment

Beijing is located at the northwest end of the North China Plain. It is surrounded by Hebei Province, except for the eastern and southeastern corners, which are bordered with Tianjin Municipality. Its terrain is descending from the northwest to southeast. It has a typical semi-humid warm continental monsoon climate, with an average temperature of -10~-5 °C in January and 22~26 °C in July, and an average annual rainfall between 500~700 mm.

Places of Interest

Beijing is one of the seven major ancient cities in China, boasting a history of more than 3000 years. The Peking Man, found in Zhoukoudian and dating back to 500,000 years ago, is the earliest origin of the ethnic groups in the Central Plains. Kublai Khan of the Yuan dynasty (1279–

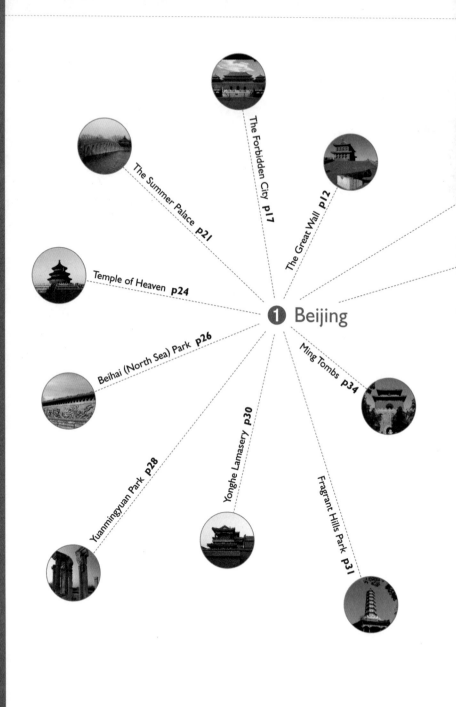

The Forbidden City **p17**

The Summer Palace **p21**

The Great Wall **p12**

Temple of Heaven **p24**

1 Beijing

Beihai (North Sea) Park **p26**

Ming Tombs **p34**

Yuanmingyuan Park **p28**

Yonghe Lamasery **p30**

Fragrant Hills Park **p31**

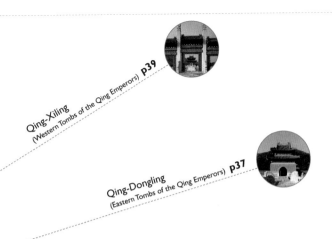

Qing-Xiling
(Western Tombs of the Qing Emperors) p39

Qing-Dongling
(Eastern Tombs of the Qing Emperors) p37

1368) constructed fortresses and dug canals to establish the Grand Capital here. The May 4 Movement (an anti-imperialist, cultural, and political movement on 1919) and the founding of New China opened a new chapter in the history and culture of the city.

Beijing has the largest number of cultural sites in China. Among them are the towering Great Wall, the glittering and splendid Imperial Palace, the vast Ming Tombs, the magnificent Temple of Heaven, Beihai Park, the Summer Palace, as well as the Zhoukoudian site of the Peking Man, the internationally renowned Lugou Bridge (Marco Polo Bridge), and the Ancient Observatory. Religious places of interest are the Biyun Temple, the Baiyun Taoist Temple, the Yonghe Lamasery and the Niujie Mosque that all have a long history of cultural significance. The alleys and quadrangle courtyards in Beijing reflect the strong style of old city.

The fame of the natural scenic spots of Beijing are carried far and wide. There are the Xiangshan Hills (Fragrant Hills) normally covered with the red leaves of maple trees in the fall, Zizhu (Purple Bamboo) Garden with exuberant bamboo woods, Yuyuantan Park with an elegant and quiet environment, Shidu Gorge in the suburbs of Beijing, Miaofeng Mountain, Longqing Gorge, and Yougu Shentan (Secluded Dell and Immortal's Pond).

The Great Wall
chang cheng

Nothing can really compare to the immense human labor that went into the construction and almost constant renovation and expansion of the greatest monument to Chinese civilization: the Great Wall.

Initiated during the Qin dynasty (221 BC–206 BC) in the 3rd century BC, when the emperor ordered the linking up of older tribal walls, the Great Wall forced into labor some 500,000 peasants, among them many convicted criminals. In the later interim and unstable rule of the Northern Wei (AD 386–AD 534), another 300,000 people were put to work on a single section south of Datong. In AD 607–AD 608, when north-south political divisions were still shaking the foundations of Chinese unity, a full 1 million people were further called upon. But all this paled against the many millions of laborers conscripted during the Ming dynasty (1368–1644) to modernize, strengthen

and extend the wall—this stage of the project alone took more than 100 years to complete.

The result is nothing short of a human marvel, a man-made protective barrier that snakes a distance of 3728 mi. (6000 km) over and through the rumpled folds of the northern Chinese landscape from Shanhaiguan Pass on the shores of the Bo Sea, through Hebei, Shanxi, Inner Mongolia, Shaanxi, Ningxia and Gansu provinces until it reaches Jiayuguan in the arid west. It is a monument to the human spirit and a memorial to immense human suffering. During each work campaign, thousand died of sickness, accident, exposure or simply the physical ordeal. Almost everything was done by hand, passing from one to another the raw materials—rock, earth, bricks, lime and site. Handcarts were used on flat land or gentle slopes, and goats and donkeys sometimes hauled the bricks and lime, but otherwise it was harsh and unremitting human toil that built this most spectacular man-made structure.

The Great Wall of the Warring States Period

Long before the Great Wall itself was built, primitive defensive mounds and walls were thrown up here and there throughout northern China to protect tribal groups from surprise attack. According to ancient records, the state of Chu built walls in the 7th century BC in the areas that are now Henan and Hubei Provinces.

The Great Wall of the Warring States emerged from several

defensive lines of tamped earth built by the various states, and it was these unconnected walls that were joined together and strengthened to form the first stage of the Great Wall in the Qin dynasty. The Qi wall was built in the 5th century BC in what is now the province of Shandong. It runs from Pingyin in the west, around the northern slopes of Tai Mountain, and ends at the coast.

Watchtowers of the Great Wall
(长城烽火台 *chang cheng feng huo tai*)

There were two types of watchtowers built along the Great Wall—*qiang tai* (wall towers), which were erected on the wall itself or jutted from its sides, and *di tai* (enemy towers), which were two-story fortifications containing living quarters and arsenals and crenellated parapets. Many of these enemy towers can still be found along a 311 mi. (500 km) section of relatively intact wall in the northern part of Hebei Province. Designed by the Ming general Qi Jiguang, they were placed at short intervals, particularly between Juyongguan Pass and Shanhaiguan Pass.

Jinshanling Wall
(金山岭长城 *jin shan ling chang cheng*)

One particularly well-defended stretch of the wall—now crumbling in many places—was built in 1570 by General Qi Jiguang to cover a series of low rolling hills at Jinshanling. Because the open, gently rising terrain gave any enemy easy access to the Han hinterland, the wall along this 19-mi. (30-km)

Admission:
5:00~17:00 (Apr. 1~Oct. 31), ¥50
7:00~17:00 (Nov.1~Mar. 31), ¥40
Tel: 0314-8830222
      0314-8830555
      0314-8830078

section was heavily strengthened and well fortified with watchtowers and beacon posts.

Juyongguan Pass
(居庸关 *ju yong guan*)

When the first emperor of Qin completed the first stage of the Great Wall's construction, he found he had another problem on his hands—many hundreds of unwanted laborers. He resettles them at Juyongguan Pass in Changping County of what is now Beijing—the name Juyong believed to be a shortened version of Xi Ju Yong Tu, meaning "to resettle redundant people."

But Juyongguan Pass has an important strategic place in history too. Flanked by high mountains and straddling a 12-mi.-long (20-km-long) gully, it was regarded as a vital linchpin in the defense of northern China and apparently so indomitable that it was the subject of at least one poetic tribute: "With only one soldier to defend the place, even ten thousand attackers will fail to capture it."

Near Juyongguan Pass there

is a platform called Yun Tai (Cloud Platform) built in 1345 of white marble. It once supported three Buddhist stupas, which were destroyed around the time of the late Yuan dynasty. A nearby monastery, Taian, built in 1439, was burned down in 1702. What is left of Yun Tai, the base, features an arched gate 23 ft (7 m) high and wide enough for a carriage to be driven through. The facade is decorated with Buddhist images which were carved there during the Ming reign.

Badaling Wall

(八达岭长城 *ba da ling chang cheng*)

The Badaling (Eight-Reaching Pass) section of the Great Wall climbs high up a mountain range in the Yanqing County of Beijing and offers one of the best surviving examples of the Wall's defensive architecture and fortification. This area of the Wall and its garrison were built in 1505 in the reign of the Ming emperor, Xiaozong, and they were definitely built to last. The wall itself is higher than most other sections, rests on huge stone slabs and is constructed almost entirely of brick and stone. The parapets are crenellated, and the lower sections of the walls have loopholes for defensive fire by arches. The top surface of the wall is 16 ft (5 m) wide, with space enough for 5 horses of 10 soldiers to march abreast along it.

Admission:
6:30~19:00 (Apr. 1~Oct. 31),
¥45
7:00~18:00 (Nov. 1~Mar. 31),
¥40
Tel: 010-69121268
www.badaling.gov.cn

Admission:
7:30~17:00 (Apr. 1~Oct. 31),
¥45/Adult ¥25/Student
8:00~17:00 (Nov. 1~Mar. 31),
¥40/Adult ¥22.5/Student
Tel: 010-69771665

The Forbidden City

gu gong

Better known all over the world as Beijing's Forbidden City, the Ancient Palaces were the residence and political nerve center of the emperors of the Ming and succeeding Qing dynasties, and the hotbed of intrigue among their huge courts. The original palaces, which took 15 years to build, were started in 1406 by the third emperor of the Ming dynasty, Chengzu, when he moved the imperial capital to Beijing. The complex, the largest surviving cluster of wooden buildings on such a scale in the world, has since played a central role in the most momentous phases of contemporary Chinese history—the wealth, power and glory of the Ming, the Manchu triumph of the Qing dynasty (1644–1911), then its gradual decay in the face of foreign pressure and incursion, and finally the complete collapse of the dynastic order. After the fall of the Qing and establishment of the short-lived Chinese republic, the Forbidden City fell into disrepair but was restored in the 1950s according to its original

plans—the spirits of 24 great and not-so-great divine rulers of China's immense past still facing south, according to ancient Chinese geomancy, and their people facing north in obeisance.

The Forbidden City is girdled by a 10-m-high city wall and a 52-m-wide moat. It measures 961m long from north to south and 753 m wide from east to west, covering 780,000 sq.m. There is a gate on each side of the rectangular city wall. The layout of the architecture's complex within the city all centers on the north-south axis and sprawls eastward and westward. The architecture's red walls, golden glazed tiles, engraved beams, painted rafters rival in magnificence.

The Palace Museum was founded in 1925 to oversee the protection of the existing relics and artifacts in the collections of the Forbidden City.

Wu Men
(午门 wu men)

The gigantic terrace, on which stand the Five Phoenix Mansions, is the main front entrance to the Forbidden

City. Wu Men (Meridian Gate) is where the emperors issued edicts, had miscreant mandarins publicly flogged and presided over the execution of common criminals sharp at noon. Built in 1420 and rebuilt in 1647, it is actually five gateways, the central one reserved for the emperor's carriages. Once inside,

visitors and emissaries proceeded to the Hall of Supreme Harmony (Taihe Dian), where the rulers conducted state ceremonies and political business, or to the Hall of Preserving Harmony (Baohe Dian), which was the setting for state banquets and, at one time, the examination hall for civil service candidates. Another mansion, Hall of Central Harmony (Zhonghe Dian), was where the emperors studied briefing papers before attending meetings in the Taihe Hall. An inner section of the palaces, north of Baohe Hall, included the emperor's living quarters and Imperial Garden.

Corner Pavilion
(角楼 *jiao lou*)

The Forbidden City was so called because the common people were forbidden to enter it, and observation and security towers placed at each corner of the 1.6-million-sq. ft (150,000-sq.-m) palace grounds made certain that all but the aristocracy were kept out. These pavilions were based on the designs of the Yellow Crane and Prince Teng mansions of the Song dynasty (AD 960–1279), and today their complex and extravagant roof structures are regarded as yet another masterpiece of traditional architecture.

Qianqing Hall
(乾清殿 qian qing dian)

Admission:
8:30~17:00 (Apr. 1~Oct. 31),
Last Entry at 16:10, ¥60
8:30~16:30 (Nov.1~Mar.
31), Last Entry at 15:40
(Including the Clock Gallery
and Treasure Gallery), ¥40
Treasure Gallery and Clock
Gallery Require A Separate
Ticket of ¥10 Respectively
Tel: 010-65132255
www.dpm.org.cn

This Qing dynasty reception and banqueting hall also served a crucial role in the security and harmony of the dynastic order. It was where the Qing emperors chose their successors. From the time of Emperor Yongzheng, who assumed the throne in 1723, it was the custom for each ruler to write the name of his intended successor on two pieces of paper—one to be kept in his personal possession and the other secreted behind a plaque bearing the inscription "Frank and Honest." Upon the emperor's death, his closest minister would compare the two names, and if they tallied, they announced the new ruler. More than 40 mansions surround the Qianqing Hall, some of them containing the emperor's crown and robes of office and books and artworks; other being places where he held audiences with his chief scholars and advisers; and still others being used as reading rooms, medical consulting rooms and living quarters for the imperial servants, maids, concubines and palace eunuchs.

The Summer Palace
yi he yuan

The powerful and ruthless Empress Dowager (Cixi), the last real dynastic ruler of China, built the Summer Palace in 1888 on the site of a previous palace and garden that had dated from the Jin dynasty (1115–1234). The project has since been regarded as something of an extravagant folly. For one thing, the empress appropriated much of the cost of it, some 24 million taels of silver, from funds set up to modernize the Chinese navy—and was soon to see the navy, or fleets of magnificent but obsolete and outgunned war junks, suffer a humiliating defeat under the guns and rockets of British iron-hulled steam-paddle warship brought from England to smash open the doors

to free trade in China. As for the Summer Palace itself, Allied Forces gutted and plundered it two years after it had been completed, and a subsequent rebuilding project only added to its vast cost. Nowadays its lake, gardens, shrines and pavilions are open to the public, along with another symbol of the Empress Dowager's stubborn extravagance, the giant Marble Boat on Kunming Lake, a stone replica of a showboat paddle steamer.

A bronze pavilion, called Pavilion of Precious Clouds, is another feature of the Summer Palace. It was cast in 1750 and reaches a height of nearly 26 ft (8 m) and weighs more than 200 tons.

The Long Gallery
(长廊 *chang lang*)

This corridor, 2400 ft (728 m) long, follows the line of the northern bank of Kunming Lake and is designed to reflect its special blend of architecture and nature in the still waters around it. Its ceiling is also painted with some 8000 "still life" compositions of flowers and scenes from famous Chinese stories and legends, and for this reason it is also called the Picture Corridor. Halfway along the gallery lies the Empress Dowager's opulent Palace Which

Dispels Clouds; further along stands the beautiful Listening to Orioles Hall (Tingliguan); and at the end of the corridor the garish white Marble Boat reflects the sudden twist of refinement to vulgarity that took place in the Empress Dowager's reign.

Kunming Lake
(昆明湖 *kun ming hu*)

A number of streams from the western districts of Beijing, including one called Jade Spring Mountain, were channeled by engineers of the Yuan dynasty to form the great lake of the Summer Palace. The Qing emperor, Qianlong, gave it its name when he refurbished a Ming dynasty palace and temple, the Duobao Pagoda, to celebrate his mother's 60th birthday. Later, the Empress Dowager added much of the rest of the construction around the lake, including the Palace Which Dispels Clouds, which she built to celebrate her own birthday.

Admission:
Gate: 6:30~18:00
(Apr. 1~Oct. 31), ¥60
Parks Inside the Summer
Palace: 8:30~17:00
Close: 20:00
Gate: 7:00~17:00
(Nov. 1~Mar.31), ¥50
Parks Inside the Summer
Palace: 9:00~16:00
Close: 19:00
Tel: 010-62881144
www.summerpalace-china.
com

Temple of Heaven

tian tan

Tiantan, the Temple of Heaven, in the southwestern corner of Beijing, is an ensemble of shines and was once the venue for the most important imperial rite— prayers for good harvest, sacrifices to the gods and royal ancestors and communion with the heavens. Built in 1420 (the 18th year of the reign of the Ming emperor Yongle), the building is part of a series of four temples in Beijing representing the firmament, the others being the Temple of the Sun, the Temple of the Earth and the Temple of the Moon. The buildings are spaced out over an area of more than 29.4 million sq. ft (2,700,000 sq. m), and altogether took 14 years to build.

The Temple of Heaven consists of two main structures linked by an 1188-ft-long (360-m-long) bridge. It is regarded as the most remarkable architectural composition, in which mathematical balance and economy

of design have achieved an almost overwhelming majesty. It is also a masterpiece of acoustics, its most novel feature being a circular wall of polished bricks in Huangqiong House (Imperial Vault of Heaven), where echoes run clearly from one end to another, giving it the name Echo Wall. This hall also contains sacred ancestral tablets, as well as those dedicated to the gods of rain, the sun, the moon, the stars, dawn, wind, thunder and lightning. When Western troops invaded Beijing in 1860 and 1900, the Temple of Heaven suffered serious damage, and it was not until 1918 that the temple was repaired and reopened to the public.

Qiniandian
（祈年殿 *qi nian dian*）

The Temple for Praying for a Good Harvest with a detail of its domed ceiling, dominates the Temple of Heaven from the top of three concentric terraces fenced with carved white marble balustrades. It is where the emperor came each year at the first full moon for fertility rites that go back to the distant beginnings of Chinese history. At the winter solstice he would also mount the three terraces of the Circular Sacrificial Altar where, after much prayer and traditional clay pipe music, a young bullock would be sacrificed to the gods. As such, the emperor was the vital conduit between the teeming Chinese society and the spiritual forces that ruled much of its existence. Though sometimes a harsh and despotic ruler himself, he was also servant of two masters—acting as vehicle through which the people's fears and wishes were made known to the heavenly deities, and a kind of human lightning rod for bolts of good fortune or retribution from on high.

Admission:
The Park: 6:00~21:00
Major Sightseeing Spots:
8:00~17:30 (Mar.1~Jun.30),
8:00~18:00 (Jul.1~Oct.31),
8:00~17:00 (Nov.1~Feb.28)
¥35 (Apr.1~Oct. 31), ¥30
(Nov.1~Mar. 31)
Tel: 010-67028866

Beihai (North Sea) Park

bei hai gong yuan

For more than 1000 years the Beihai Park—as mundane as its name may be—was the royal garden of successive dynasties that included the Liao (AD 916–1125), Jin (1125–1234), Yuan and Ming. It covers an area of 7.6 million sq. ft (700,000 sq. m), and among its beautifully landscaped gardens, hillocks and pools there are two particular artistic attractions. One, the famous Nine Dragon Wall, is an 86-ft-long (26-m-long) ceramic monument made up of 424 seven-colored glazed tiles depicting nine dragons in high relief on each side. The other showpiece is the White Stupa (or Dagoba), which is a prime example of Tibetan Buddhist architecture. Built in 1651, it was badly damaged by earthquakes in 1679 and 1731.

Quiet Mind Studio of Qianlong
(静心斋 *jing xin zhai*)

Nature and the architect's vision have blended splendidly to create this garden within a garden, originally called Jingxinzhai, or Quiet Mind Studio, on the northern shore of Beihai in Beijing. It features elaborate formations of rocks from Lake Tai in artificial hills and craggy shorelines around the garden's lotus and lily covered ponds, and a series of peaceful pavilions and water bowers. Constructed in 1758, Quiet Mind Studio was completely renovated in 1913 after the fall of the dynastic order and was used as a reception venue for foreign diplomats.

Admission:
6:00~20:30 (April, May, September, and October)
6:00~22:00 (June, July, and August)
6:00~20:00 (January, February, March, November and December)
¥5/Adult, ¥2/Student
Tel: 010-64040610
www.beihaipark.com.cn

Yuanmingyuan Park
yuan ming yuan

The ruins of Yuanmingyuan Park, the imperial gardens of the Summer Palace outside Beijing, are still a famous destination in China even though few traces of its magnificent beauty remain today. In the past, the gardens were the home of the emperor and his court from the beginning of each Chinese lunar New Year in early spring until autumn. For over 150 years the gardens, bridges, pagodas and residences were the pet project of emperors who based their design on well-known scenic spots in China and other famous garden designs. The area for the gardens was already blessed with an abundance of natural springs and hills, but that was just the raw material for the creation of a fairytale landscape that exemplified the imperial desire to have all the beauty of China belong within the emperor's garden walls. Rivers, waterfalls, lakes and islands dotted the transformed landscape. The theme of each special garden site was created to represent China's cherished artistic, literary and philosophical concepts that the emperor then had the privilege of naming. The finest materials went in to the building of the garden's exquisite architecture. These marvelous structures were furnished from the vast imperial collections of art, antiques and books. As contact with the West began to influence imperial taste, Western building and art objects were added to Yuanmingyuan Park. The gardens represented the culmination

of 2000 years of Chinese garden design. Sadly, the weakened Qing dynasty in the second half of the 19th century was unable to protect China, and as foreign powers vied in Beijing for the rich spoils, the imperial gardens were eventually set on fire and the treasures looted. For many years, even after being in a disastrous state of ruin, the gardens inspired poetry describing its tragic beauty.

Admission:
7:00~18:00 (April, September, and October)
7:00~19:00 (May, June, July, and August)
7:00~17:30 (January, February, March, November and December)
¥10
Tel: 010-62637561
     010-62628501

Yonghe Lamasery

yong he gong

The Qing emperor Yongzheng lived in this complex first as a prince and later as emperor, using parts of the premises for the practice of Tibetan Buddhism. When the emperor died, his coffin was lodged here, and the green roof tiles were replaced by yellow ones, whereby the place was officially elevated to the rank of a palace for housing Yongzheng's image and for the ancestral worship of the royal Qing house. The palace was presented to the lamas by Emperor Qianlong in 1744 and turned into a lamasery, and it stands today as the largest and one of the best-preserved Buddhist institutions in China. In the five halls that make up the monastery, valuable Buddhist images in bronze and stone stand alongside rare relics of the Yellow Sect of Tibetan Buddhism, including ancient copies of the Tripitaka sutras. Its walls contain many colorful murals of Buddhist stories and Buddha images. The many side rooms also house valuable collections of Buddhist scriptures and writings in mathematics, medicine, astronomy, and geography.

Admission:
Tel: 010-64044499

30

Fragrant Hills Park

xiang shan gong yuan

This scenic park west of Beijing is a location that has been favored by imperial dynasties since the 12th century when it was chosen as an imperial hunting ground. Pavilions, temples and summer retreats for the imperial family have graced the park, but time, changes in fashion and the destruction of much imperial property in the late 19th century by foreign powers have conspired to remove many of the structures built in the park over its long history. The brilliant autumn foliage of the smoke trees that cover the hills to the west of the park has long made the park a popular destination. For the hardy admirers of nature, winter also is a favorite time to take in the beauty of snow-covered hills.

There are a number of temples in the park, including the Temple of Brilliance, a copy of a Tibetan temple. The delightful Glazed Tile Pagoda has bronze bells that tinkle in the wind and hang from the eaves of each of its seven stories. A small garden within the park was once the site of the Summer Palace. The semicircular pool surrounded by a covered walkway is similar to the original that once decorated the grounds of the Summer Palace.

Glazed Pagoda of Fragrant Hills
(多宝琉璃塔 *duo bao liu li ta*)

This beautiful green pagoda is eight-sided and seven-tiered but only 33 ft (10 m) tall. It stands in Fragrant Hills Park in Beijing and was built in typical Qing dynasty fashion, with a combination of stone tiles and wooden corridors and 56 bronze wind bells tinkling from its many eaves. It is the only structure to survive inside the Zhao Temple, which was built in 1780 (the 45th year of the reign of the Qing emperor Qianlong) in the Tibetan style of architecture, and served as a guesthouse to the 6th Panchen lama when he visited Beijing. The pagoda, which lies to the west of it, is now regarded as the emblem of this complex.

Shifangpujue Monastery
(卧佛寺 *wo fo si*)

Located on the southern slope of Shou'an Hill just outside Beijing, this monastery was first built in the Tang dynasty (AD 618–AD 907) in the 7th century and rebuilt in 1734 (the 12th year of the Qing emperor Yongzheng). It is also called the Sleeping Buddha Monastery, because it houses a reclining statue of Buddha. The main feature of this symmetrically designed monastery is the Hall of the Sleeping Buddha, where a bronze image of Sakyamuni lies in an apparent state of Nirvana. The statue, cast in 1321 in the Yuan dynasty, is more than 17 ft (5 m) long and depicts Sakyamuni speaking with his disciples about his impending departure from all earthly things. Lying on one side, with his right hand pitched against his head, the Buddha is the very picture of ease and calm, attended by disciples represented here as 12 clay statues standing behind him.

Biyun Monastery
(碧云寺 *bi yun si*)

When Buddha first took root in China, its architecture naturally followed the style of that of its birthplace, India. But almost all early Chinese construction was of wood, and the evidence of whole periods of history was destroyed by fire. Through a combination of reconstruction and its own artistic development, Han Chinese architecture soon dominated the design of religious and public buildings. A group of white marble pagodas remains, however, as a striking example of early Indian design in the Biyun Monastery on the eastern slope of Fragrant Hills or Xiangshan, in Beijing. The tallest is 13-tiered and 116 ft (35 m) high and is decorated with Tibetan Buddhist themes in bas-relief.

Admission:
6:00~18:30 (Apr.1~Jun.30)
6:00~19:00 (Jul.1~Aug.31)
6:00~18:00 (Nov.16~Mar.31)
¥10 (Apr.1~Nov.15),
¥5 (Nov.16~Mar.31), ¥10
(Biyun Monastery)
Tel: 010-62591264

Ming Tombs
ming shi san ling

Ranking with the Forbidden City and the Great Wall as one of the most renowned monuments to Chinese imperial history, the Ming tombs lie in the shadow of Tianshou Mountain 31 mi. (50 m) north of Beijing. They were built as mausoleums for 13 emperors of the Ming dynasty from reign of Chengzu to Sizong, covering a period of more than 200 years from 1409 to 1644. The approach to the tombs alone is monumental—an 11-story white marble memorial archway with five gates and six pillars is the main entrance; beyond it stands the Dahong Gate (Red Main Gate) with red walls and yellow roof tiles; and beyond that lies a wide 4-mi (7-km) Road of the Gods lined with

large stone sculptures of lions, camels, elephants, unicorns and horses and statues of court officials in the ceremonial dress, each slightly bowed in a gesture of respect. The tombs of the emperors and their consorts are found in the Baocheng (Precious) City, each surrounded by a red wall and each containing a particular stone

tablet that, unlike the others, has nothing inscribed upon it —symbolizing the infinite beneficence of the imperial rulers.

Chang Tomb
(长陵 *chang ling*)

No other tomb ranks in size and grandeur with the Chang Tomb, built in 1409 for the emperor Yongle. Its Lingen Hall stands on a 10-ft-(3-m-) high white marble podium. It covers an area of 20,452 sq. ft (1900 sq. m) and is supported by 60 timber columns that, five centuries later, are every bit as sturdy and well preserved as when they were first installed. Chang Tomb is the first mausoleum to have been built, and it set the standard of design for the 12 other tombs that followed.

Ding Tomb
(定陵 *ding ling*)

Lying southwest of Chang Tomb below the Dayu Hill, Ding Tomb was built for Emperor Shenzong and his two queens. Started in 1548 when he was still alive, it was completed six years later. It features the Brilliant

Tower, roofed with yellow-glazed cylindrical tiles and stone tablets inscribed with the words *da ming* (Great Ming) and Tomb of Shenzong, but otherwise there is little surface evidence of the far grander spectacle that lies under the ground behind this mausoleum entrance.

The Underground Palace
(地宫 *di gong*)

Right behind the Brilliant Tower of Ding Tomb lies the Underground Palace, or burial tomb, of Emperor Shenzong and his two queens, the only burial hall excavated so far in the Ming Tombs. Archeologists broke through to it in 1956 and found five chambers, each separated by a 4-ton stone door, that were as majestic as any of the Pharaonic tombs unearthed in Egypt.

Under the vast domed ceiling of the stone hall they found the coffins of Shenzong and his wives, along with golden crowns the other ceremonial headwear, porcelain, utensils, jade vases, silk wear and other burial possessions—the stone funerary bed lying in surroundings of bare simplicity compared with the décor and furnishings of the adjoining chambers. There, the floors are paved with "gold" tiles impregnated with tung oil to give them a lasting luster, and the central chamber features intricately carved white marble benches, blue porcelain urns with dragon motifs and other Ming dynasty artwork.

Admission:
6:30~18:00 (Apr. 1~Oct. 31)
7:00~17:00 (Nov. 1~Mar.31)
Dingling Tomb: ¥40 (Nov. 1~Mar.31), ¥60 (Apr. 1~Oct. 31)
Changling Tomb: ¥30 (Nov. 1~Mar.31), ¥45 (Apr. 1~Oct. 31)
Zhaoling Tomb: ¥20 (Nov. 1~Mar.31), ¥30 (Apr. 1~Oct. 31)
Sacred Way: ¥20 (Nov. 1~Mar.31), ¥30 (Apr. 1~Oct. 31)
Tel: Dingling Tomb
　　010-60761424
　　Changling Tomb
　　010-60761888
　　Zhaoling Tomb
　　010-60763104
　　Sacred Way
　　010-89749383

Qing-Dongling (Eastern Tombs of the Qing Emperors)

qing dong ling

The Qing dynasty buried its emperors on a series of sites, the earliest of them in Zunhua County, 78 mi. (125 km) east of Beijing, named Dongling—a cluster of mausoleums that developed into the most extensive burial spot in China. The tombs were commenced in 1663, and emperors Shunzhi, Kangxi, Qianlong, Xianfeng and Tongzhi, along with their consorts and more that 100 concubines were laid to rest. Though not as ornate as the preceding Ming dynasty tombs, these burial places followed basically the same pattern of Great Red Gate entrances opening on to sacred avenues—a 3.7-mi. (6-km) approach in this

case—lined with stone sculptures of animals and statues of civil and military officers.

Yu Mausoleum
(裕陵 *yu ling*)

The largest of the Qing-Dongling is that of Emperor Shunzhi, but the most impressive are those of Qianlong (Yu Mausoleum) and the Emperess Dowager Cixi. The underground palace of Yu Mausoleum is composed of nine arches and four gates totaling 54 m in length starting from the first stone gate, all the walls and arches are carved with Buddhist topics. The carvings, exquisite and smooth, are vivid to life and carefully patterned.

Admission:
8:00~17:00 (Apr. 1~Oct. 31)
8:30~16:30 (Nov. 1~Mar.31)
¥120/Adult, ¥60/Student
Tel: 0315-6944467
　　0315-6944383
　　0315-6945475
　　0315-6945471

Qing-Xiling (Western Tombs of the Qing Emperors)

qing xi ling

The other Qing dynasty monarchs were buried in the Qing-Xiling, a resting place covering 598,000 sq. yd (500,000 sq. m) in Yi county, Hebei. The whole mausoleum complex contains the tombs of four Qing emperors (Yongzheng, Jiaqing, Daoguang and Guangxu), three empress, seven princes and a number of imperial concubines. The tombs here are more scattered than those at Qing-Dongling but are considered architecturally more interesting and are set against a pleasant backdrop of wooded hills.

Admission:
8:30~17:30 (Apr. 1~Oct. 31)
8:30~17:00 (Nov. 1~Mar.31)
¥122/Adult, ¥62/Student
Tel: 0312-4710012
　　 0312-4710016
　　 0312-4710038

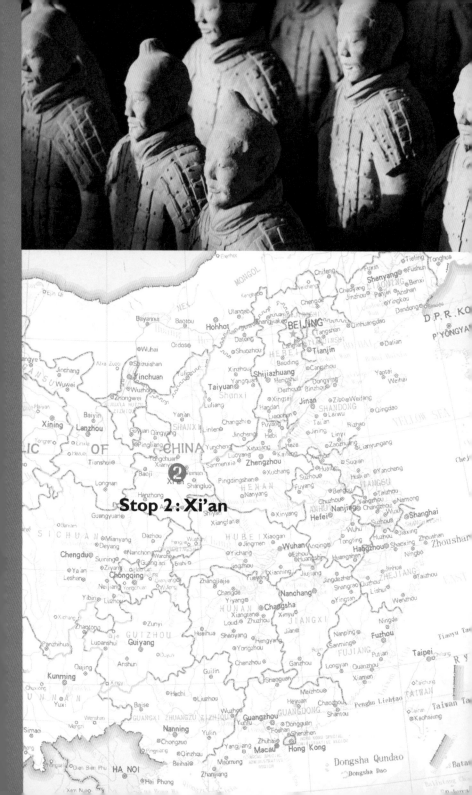

Stop 2: Xi'an

Get Started Here

General Information

Xi'an is the Provincial capital of Shaanxi Province in the central-northwest region of China. As one of the seven ancient capitals of China, it was the capital of 13 dynasties from the time of the 11th century BC rule of the Western Zhou (c.1046 BC–c.771 BC) to the triumph of the Tang (AD 618–AD 907). Xi'an is also known for being the eastern terminal of the Silk Road and the location of the terra-cotta army.

Environment

It is located in the hinterland of China, at the lower reaches of the Yellow River. It is surrounded by the Qinling Mountains and Weihe River. The continental climate makes it cold and dry in winter. Except for the winter, any season is relatively suitable for travel. The average temperature is 0℃ or above in January and around 25℃ in July, with an average annual rainfall between 500~800 mm.

Places of Interest

"The 5,000-year history of China is mirrored in Xi'an." Shaanxi is one of the most important cradles where the Chinese civilization was concentrated. As early as 1 million years ago, the Lantian Man settled down and lived there. In this "natural history museum," there are not only the relics of the ancient Chang'an City, the legendary tomb of Emperor Huangdi, the Qianling Mausoleum, Maoling, the Tomb of Wudi of the Han

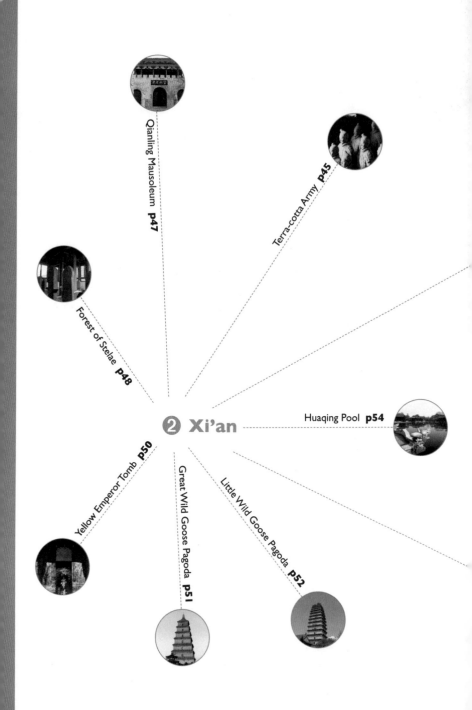

Qianling Mausoleum **p47**

Terra-cotta Army **p45**

Forest of Stelae **p48**

❷ **Xi'an**

Huaqing Pool **p54**

Yellow Emperor Tomb **p50**

Great Wild Goose Pagoda **p51**

Little Wild Goose Pagoda **p52**

Xi'an City Wall **p44**

dynasty (206 BC–AD 220), but also the Forest of Stelae, Huaqing Pool, and the Great Wild Goose Pagoda. The once buried terra-cotta warriors and horses are one of the world's great wonders.

The northern Shaanxi Plateau features the typical Loess Plateau arts and customs, the classic and sonorous Xintianyou folksong, the energetic and brisk waist-drum dancing, delicate paper cutting, and the novelty-rich Chinese peasant painting.

The natural landscape of Shaanxi is equally unmatched. There is the West Sacred Mountain of Huashan, Lishan Mountain in Lintong, Tiantai Mountain in Baoji, Yellow Emperor Tomb, Qiachuan in Heyang, and the torrential Hukou Waterfall of the Yellow River. The river was described by famous poet Li Bai this way—"See how the Yellow River's water pours down from heaven."

www.xian-tourism.co

Drum Tower **p53**

Xi'an City Wall

xi an cheng qiang

From the 3rd century BC, Xi'an was a vital commercial center because of its position on the eastern stretches of the Silk Road. Its trading importance and its vulnerability—lying in the path of the main Central Asian conduit into the heart of central China—also made it one of the most heavily fortified cities of the north.

From its earliest days, a defensive wall encircled it, and in 1374 when the large program of defensive works was undertaken by the Ming, the city's present wall was built—a massive stone structure, strengthened with fortifications, running about 7 mi. (12 km) around Xi'an, rising 40 ft (12 m) high and spreading 45 to 60 ft (14 to 18 m) thick at its base. They include some 98 watchtowers and nearly 6000 crenels cut into a parapet that runs right around the top of the wall. There are four huge gates, over which the Ming dynasty engineers built small multistory forts with observation points and firing ports, from which teams of archers and other defenders could shower the attacking forces with arrows, gunpowder bombs and blazing oil and naphtha.

Admission:
South Gate: 8:00~20:30 (Mar.1~Apr.30), 8:00~21:30 (May.1~Oct.30), 8:00~19:00 (Nov.1~Feb.28)
Moon City: 8:00~20:30 (May.1~Oct.15), 8:00~18:00 (Oct.16~Apr.30)
Wenchang Gate: 8:00~20:00 (May.1~Oct.15), 8:00~18:00 (Oct.16~Apr.30)
Heping Gate (Peace Gate): 8:00~21:00 (May.1~Oct.15), 8:00~18:00 (Oct.16~Apr.30)
East, West, North Gate: 8:00~20:00 (May.1~Oct.15), 8:00~18:00 (Oct.16~Apr.30)
Shangde Gate, Small South Gate: 8:00~18:00 (All Year Round)
¥40
Tel: 029-87289791

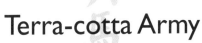

Terra-cotta Army
bing ma yong

The vast tomb of Emperor Qin Shihuang, the first Chinese emperor to unify China's warring clans 2000 years ago, might never have been discovered since its highly skilled designers had hidden it extremely well. There is some evidence that long ago grave robbers inadvertently set fires in their search for treasures, but the tomb commissioned by Emperor Qin Shihuang lay quietly 15 to 20 ft (4.5 to 6.5 m) below the Earth's surface, covered by a roof built with layers of fiber mats followed by many feet of soil to conceal it. There is speculation that the tombs workers and supervisors were buried alive at completion to protect its secrets. In 1974 peasants near Xi'an uncovered evidence of the tomb's fabulous terra-cotta

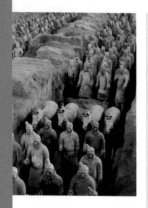

Admission:
8:30~17:30 (Mar.16~Nov.14),
8:30~17:00 (Nov.15~Mar.15)
¥90 (Mar.1~Nov.30), ¥65
(Dec.1~Feb.28)
Tel: 029-81399001
www.bmy.com.cn

army when digging a well. Their well excavation was over an area of the tomb with more than 8000 life-size terra-cotta warriors. The warriors' infinitely varied details of facial features, hair, dress, rank, and the horses for cavalry divisions meant that no two were alike. The figures had been fired at higher than usual temperatures for terra-cotta and were shaped by using cleverly carved molds to allow for hollow torsos, heads and arms. The legs were solid terra-cotta needed to support each figure's overall weight of up to 600 lb (300 kg). Experts believe this terra-cotta army is only a small part of the buried treasures of Emperor Qin Shihuang's tomb since it lies approximately less than a mi. (1000 m) east of the main tomb. The main entrance to the tomb has still not been located even to this day.

Qianling Mausoleum

qian ling

Magnificent stone lions guard the entrance to this, the burial place of Emperor Gaozong and Empress Wu of the Tang dynasty. The mausoleum, hewn out of three hills, lies at Liang Mountain in Qian County, Shaanxi. Besides the stone lions, ostriches, winged horses and soldiers that surround the tomb, there are statues of 61 leaders of regional ethnic minorities and foreign diplomats of that time. Emperor Gaozong died in AD 684, and his queen 22 years later.

Admission:
8:00~20:00
¥46 (Mar.16~Nov.14), ¥26 (Nov.15~Mar.15)
Tel: 0910-5510222

Forest of Stelae
bei lin

In the Tang dynasty, when Xi'an was called Chang'an, the city was noted for its large collection of stone stele, many of them featuring fine examples of early Chinese calligraphy or carvings of the 13 Classics of Confucian philosophy. In the year AD 904, it was decided that the entire collection should be brought under one roof, so to speak, and a place was reserved within the city wall. But it took another 186 years for work to be completed on Xi'an's Forest of Stelae, a sprawling complex of exhibition halls, covered corridors and a pavilion, which nowadays houses more than 1000 stelaes and tomb tablets.

The exhibition virtually encompasses the history of Chinese writing, presenting the calligraphy of the Qin

dynasty (221 BC–206 BC) of the 3rd century BC, through the Tang and Song and into the Ming and final Qing reigns. In 1555 powerful earthquake caused extensive damage to the halls, and the complex was rebuilt at the end of that century. Three new halls were added during the 17th and 18th centuries.

The impressive collection includes all the representative styles of Chinese calligraphy, such as the ancient official script, the highly abstract cursive script and the artistic writings of the great painter-poets, all of which became models for later students of calligraphy. Some of the stelae on display are of great historical value, such as the stela recording the introduction of Christianity into China. Another remarkable stela is a bas-relief called the Four Steeds of Zhao Mausoleum. It is in fact the tombstone of Taizong, the second emperor of the Tang dynasty, and shows the four splendid warhorses that he rode in campaigns against the northern "ethnic minority groups."

Admission:
8:00~18:45(Summer),
8:00~18:00(Winter)
¥45 (Mar.16~Nov.14), ¥30
(Nov.15~Mar.15)
Tel: 0910-87210764

Yellow Emperor Tomb

huang di ling

The Yellow Emperor is credited with being the father of traditional Chinese medicine, the inventor of agriculture and the father of the Chinese race itself. His tomb in Qiaoshan in Huangling County, Shaanxi, was built in the Song dynasty to replace an earlier monument set up in the time of the Han. At the foot of a hill close to the tomb there are 14 cedar trees, one of which is said in legend to have been planted by the Yellow Emperor himself. A large plaque in the main hall bears the inscription First Ancestor of Humanity.

Admission:
8:00~19:00
¥91 (Mar.16~Nov.14),
¥51 (Nov.15~Mar.15)
Tel: 0911-5212742

Great Wild Goose Pagoda
da yan ta

This magnificent pagoda south of Xi'an was built by the Buddhist monk Xuanzang (AD 602–AD 664) to store the sutras that he brought from India during the first flowering of the religion in China. The pagoda takes its name from a compelling incident, recorded in Tripitaka's biography, in which a flock of wild geese flew over a monastery in Magadha, a kingdom in Central India. One of them broke its wings and fell from the sky. The monks, believing that it was a Bodhisttva, buried the goose and built the pagoda in its honor.

Admission:
8:00~19:00
¥25 (¥20 for the tower)
Tel: 029-85535014
www.xiandayanta.com

The pagoda had only five stories when it was first built, and two others were added in the time of the Five dynasties. It bears inscriptions by the Tang emperors Taizong and Gaozong. During their reigns it was customary for successful candidates in the civil service examinations to be entertained at the nearby Apricot Garden and then taken to the Great Wild Goose Pagoda for their signing ceremony. It became a great honor for scholars to "sign at the Great Wild Goose Pagoda," and the poet Bai Juyi (AD 772–AD 846) went one step further than that: "Of those who signed beneath the Great Wild Goose Pagoda, seventeen in all," he wrote, "I was the youngest."

Little Wild Goose Pagoda

xiao yan ta

Admission:
8:00~17:00
¥18, ¥12 (¥50 for tower)
Tel: 029-87802070
029-87892313
029-87811081
www.xaxyt.com

Located in Jianfu monastery, close to the southern gate of Xi'an, the Little Wild Goose Pagoda has a most tumultuous history—it has been struck by no less than 70 earthquakes since it was first built in the year AD 707 and has survived every one of them. According to the city's records, one of the tremors in 1487 was so violent that it left a split 1ft (a third of meter) wide right down the middle of the tower. But 34 years later it was struck—and this time the action of the quake closed the crack. But the pagoda hasn't survived completely unscathed. It was originally 15 stories high, but earthquakes destroyed the two top floors.

In Jianfu Monastery there hangs a large bell that was cast and installed in the Ming dynasty. A beautiful poem pays tribute to its toll:

Frost accompanies the grayish break of dawn,

On which is painted the still dallying moon.

My dream is broken by the sound of the monastery bell,

Which for ten centuries haunted the mystic air.

Drum Tower

gu lou

While Western medieval towns and forts had night-watch sentries to call the hours of the night, a large drum on the upper floor of this two-story tower in Xi'an boomed out the coming of darkness. The Drum Tower was built in 1380 in the reign of the Ming emperor Taizu and was renovated twice in the following centuries. It is remarkably well preserved and is one of the historic showpieces of a city whose name is synonymous with Chinese history.

Admission:
9:00~17:00
¥27
Tel: 029-87274580

Huaqing Pool
hua qing chi

One of the eight most celebrated places of natural beauty in Central China, Huaqing Pool is also the location of a hot springs system that is steeped in history and legend. The first Qin emperor is said to have built a traveling lodge beside the springs, which are found on the slope of Mount Li in the south of Lintong County. According to folklore, on one of his visits, he encountered

an immortal disguised as a common peasant woman, who, taking exception to his rather familiar behavior toward her, spat in his face. The emperor's features immediately broke out in a dreadful skin ailment. Apologizing profusely for his indiscretions, the emperor begged her to remove the curse— and the woman revealed herself as an immortal and bathed his face in the spring, curing him as swiftly as he has been afflicted. Thereafter, the hot springs of Mount Li were known as the Immortal Hot Springs.

Another of the springs, called Hibiscus, became the trysting spot of the Tang emperor Xuanzong and his beautiful concubine Yang. The poet Bai Juyi, in his poem *Song of Everlasting Woe*, describes how the "streams of the warm fountain caressed her waxen limbs."

Admission:
8:00~16:00
¥70 (Mar.1~Nov.30), ¥40
(Dce.1~Feb.28)
Tel: 029-83812003
www.hqc.cn

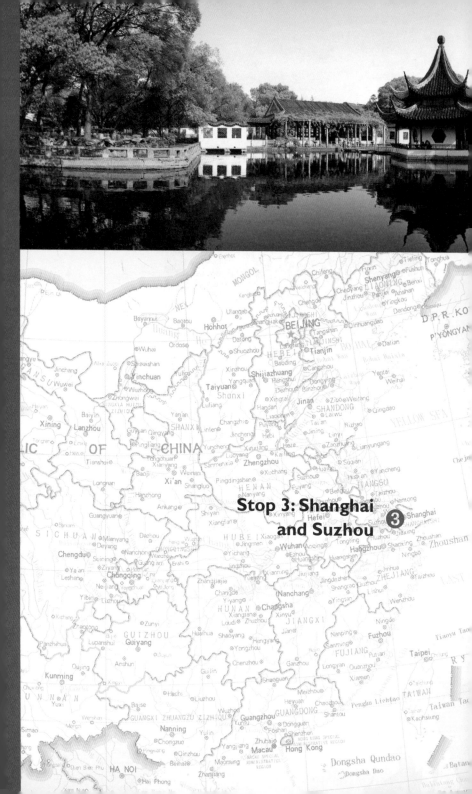

Stop 3: Shanghai and Suzhou ③

Suzhou
Get Started Here

General Information

Suzhou is one of the oldest cities on the lower reaches of the Yangtze River and on the shores of Taihu Lake in Jiangsu Province.

A large area of the city is covered by water, including a vast number of ponds and streams. Taihu Lake, four-fifths of which is in the territory of Suzhou, is one of the four largest fresh lakes in China. The city is cut by the Beijing-Hangzhou Grand Canal from north to south.

Since the Song dynasty, Suzhou has been an important center for China's silk industry and continues to hold that prominent position today.

Environment

About 80%~90% of Jiangsu Province's territory are plains, the lowest and flattest land in China. Suzhou is influenced by the northern subtropical humid monsoon climate. The average temperature is 2~8 ℃ in January and 26~32 ℃ in July, with an average annual rainfall between 800~1,200 mm.

Places of Interest

Suzhou is an ancient city with a 2500 years' history. It's "a very great and noble city ... It has 1600 stone bridges under which a galley may pass." (Marco Polo) Strolling on the streets, you can feel the unique charm left by its long legacy.

Suzhou's classic gardens reveal the heart and soul of the city. The

Taihu Lake **p60**

Tiger Hill Pagoda **p62**

Han Shan Monastery **p61**

Humble Administrator's Garden **p63**

3
Suzhou

Lion Forest Garden **p64**

Master-of-Nets Garden **p66**

Couple's Garden Retreat **p65**

Garden of Cultivation **p69**

classic gardens—full of poetic and artistic expression by traditional Chinese freehand brushwork paintings—are made through the elaborate arrangement of rocks, water, vegetation, and layout of the buildings. These gardens were named UNESCO World Heritage Sites in 1997 and 2000. At present, more than 60 gardens are kept intact here.

The exquisite water townships in Suzhou are rated by tourists alongside classical gardens. Zhouzhuang, Mudu, Tongli towns should not be missed by any visitor. In any water township of Suzhou, a number of Ming and Qing dynasties preserved buildings can be found. The natural scenery and human landscape enhance each other's beauty, providing a peaceful oasis for visitors.

Lingering Garden **p68**

West Garden **p67**

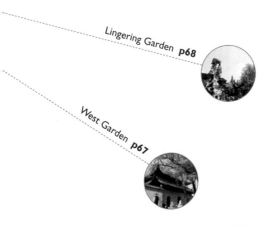

Taihu Lake

tai hu

The Taihu Lake is the third biggest freshwater lake in China and is famous for its rocks—strange and somewhat bizarre natural formations that have been used all over China to decorate parks and gardens. It is also where Fan Li, the mastermind who help the Prince of Yue to inflict vengeance on the Prince of Wu in 476 BC, is said to have celebrated his victory by taking the most coveted beauty of that time, Xi Shi, for a boat ride. The lake covers 926 sq. mi. (2400 sq. km) and spreads into the provinces of Jiangsu and Zhejiang. It is mainly fed by two streams, the Tiao and Jing and empties through many others into the Yangtze River. There are 48 small islands in its waters, and peaks of 72 hills parade around it.

Han Shan Monastery
han shan si

Han Shan Monastery in Fengqiao, Suzhou, dates back to AD 502–AD 519, but was destroyed by fire several times over the centuries, and its present structure goes back only to the beginning of this century. Its name is said to have come from the monk Han Shan, who came to the area with a colleague, Shi De. Gilded statues of both men are housed in its great hall. The Tang dynasty poet Zhang Ji immortalized the monastery in lines that spoke of "the sound of the midnight bell (coming) to my lonely boat." The monastery bell disappeared a long time ago, and a replacement installed in the Ming dynasty has also gone—it is now in a collection in Japan. A new one hangs in Han Shan monastery, which was made in Japan and donated to the monastery.

Admission:
7:00~17:30
¥20
Tel: 0512-65336634

Tiger Hill Pagoda
hu qiu

Built in the middle of the 10th century on Tiger Hill in Suzhou, the eight-sided seven-tiered tapering pagoda is constructed of bricks but in the style of traditional wooden structures. In 700 years, from the 12th to 19th centuries, it suffered seven major fires that badly damaged the top and all the eaves. What remains now is the basic brick structure, which requires constant maintenance. First named the Yunyan Pagoda, it is probably the oldest of its design south of the Yangtze River. The pagoda stands 164 ft (50 m) high, and every floor is accessible by a wooden staircase.

On every story of the pagoda, there are murals of peonies. Other features, such as the cantilevered brackets and coffered ceilings, are also painted over with rather special designs.

Admission:
7:30~17:00
¥60 (Apr.16~Oct.30), ¥40 (Oct.31~Apr.15)
Tel: 0512-65323488
www.tigerhill.com

Humble Administrator's Garden

zhuo zheng yuan

Admission:
7:30~17:30
¥70 (Apr.16~Oct.30), ¥50 (Oct.31~Apr.15)
Tel: 0512-67510286
www.szzzy.cn

Tips:
A portable e-guide can be rented at the entrance. After you leave the Humble Administrator's Garden, a 100-m walk to the west will take you to the Royal Prince House of the Taiping Heavenly Kingdom, the Suzhou Museum, and the Suzhou Gardens Museum. Walk another 100 m south along the Garden Road to get to the Lion Forest Garden and the Suzhou Folk Culture Museum.

Another famous Suzhou residence, the Humble Administrator's Garden, was built in 1513 by a retired civil servant, Wang Xianchen, on the site of the former Dahong Monastery. He took its name from a poem on leisurely living by Pan Yue of the Jin dynasty, a line from which goes: "To water the garden and grow vegetables is a form of government by the simple soul." Renovated in the Qing reign, this is now the largest and most splendid residential garden in Suzhou. Since its first occupant, it has had some illustrious owner-residents, including the grandfather of the novelist Cao Xueqing (author of *Dream of the Red Mansion*) and Li Xiucheng, a leader of the Taiping Revolution against Qing rule.

Lion Forest Garden
shi zi lin

Admission:
7:30~17:00
¥30 (Apr.16~Oct.30), ¥20
(Oct.31~Apr.15)
Tel: 0512-67773263
      0512-67272428
www.szszl.com

Tips:
The Lion Forest Garden
is near the Suzhou Folk
Culture Museum and the
Museum of Banknotes and
Coins. You can tour these
two places together with
the Garden. A 100-m walk
to the north will take you to
the Humble Administrator's
Garden.

Lying adjacent to Humble Administrator's Garden and covering an area of 1.1 hectare, the garden was first constructed in the 2nd year of Zhizheng in the Yuan dynasty (1342). Its name came from the Buddhist doctrine. Both Emperor Kangxi and Emperor Qianlong of the Qing dynasty paid several visits to the garden and made a replica of it respectively in the Yuanmingyuan Garden of Beijing and the Mountain Resort of Chengde. The impressive and labyrinthine artificial limestone rockworks in the garden boast deep caverns and zigzagging paths. The whole garden is compactly laid out with corridors leading to all directions and small paths opening upon an enchanting view. It has also tall and graceful ancient trees.

Couple's Garden Retreat

ou yuan

The Couple's Garden Retreat has three sides facing water, with the eastern side facing the river. With the canal running through both front and back, this garden retains the classical characteristics of Suzhou Jiangnan water towns. The exterior of the Couple's Garden Retreat is the best-preserved in Suzhou. Shen Bingcheng, the founder of the Couple's Garden Retreat, resigned under the pretext of illness and moved to Suzhou with his young wife Yan, where he rebuilt the Couple's Garden Retreat on the site of a garden from the early Qing dynasty which had gone to waste.

Unlike other residential gardens that separate residential and scenic parts, the residential part of the Couple's Garden Retreat is in the center of the garden with two separate gardens situated on the east and west sides, to signify husband and wife. It is the only example of a dozen buildings being interconnected by winding walkways.

Admission:
8:00~17:00
¥25 (Apr.16~Oct.30), ¥15
(Oct.31~Apr.15)
Tel: 0512-67272717

Tips:
The Couple's Garden
Retreat, the East Garden
and the Zoo are offered as a
combination tour.

Master-of-Nets Garden

wang shi yuan

Admission:
7:30~17:30 (Mar.1~Nov.15)
7:30~7:00 (Nov.16~Feb.29)
¥30 (Apr.16~Oct.30); ¥20
(Oct.31~Apr.15)
Night Garden: 19:30~21:00
(Mar.10~Nov.20), ¥80
Tel: 0512-65293190
www.szwsy.com

Tips:
An Evening Garden Tour
is one unusual feature
of this garden. Classical
entertainment such as
Kunqu Opera and traditional
storytelling are offered. You
can view traditional stringed
and woodwind Jiangnan
(south of the Yangtze River)
instruments such as the
Guzheng and bamboo flutes
on display in the various halls
around the garden.

Suzhou has for centuries been known as one of central China's most beautiful cities and the place where wealthy mandarins, merchants and landowners built fine retirement residences, many of them connected to the network of lakes and canals that have given the city the reputation of being the Venice of the East. Master-of-Nets Garden, a particularly well-designed and opulent garden home, was built by Shi Zhengzhi of the Song dynasty and was named Ten Thousand Volumes Hall at first. In 1736 it was bought by Song Zongyuan, who changed its name to Fisherman's Recluse and chose Wang Shi (Master of Nets) as the name of its garden. With its cottages, pavilions, studios and ponds, it embodied all that the wealthy retired required of life—visual pleasure and harmony.

West Garden

xi yuan

This palatial residence complex and garden in Liuyuan Street, Suzhou, has a colorful and complicated history. First built between 1522 and 1566 by a retired Ming dynasty mandarin, it was then converted to a monastery by his son; then, in the 19th century, it was demolished and rebuilt in its present form. It still includes the monastery, and a main hall that houses the images of 500 arhats and a statue of the monk Ji Gong, whose face, viewed from the right, has an amused, happy expression, but from the left is sad. Viewed from the front, it appears to be happy and sad all at once. The pond that links the various buildings is well stocked with colorful carp and is home to a tortoise said to be over 300 years old.

Admission:
¥25
Tel: 0512-65525145

Lingering Garden
liu yuan

Located outside of the Changmen Gate and covering an area of 2.3 hectare, it is one of the four most famous gardens in China. A retired bureaucrat first constructed the garden during the reign of Wanli (1573–1620) in the Ming dynasty and then it was renovated during the late period in the Qing dynasty. The garden is celebrated for its exquisite and artistic division of architectural space with halls, corridors, whitewashed walls and tunnel portals. The seemingly divided areas, combined with stones, water and vegetation, form a variety of interlocking courts, which exhibits an artistic feature of gardens south of the lower Yangtze.

The Lingering Garden is divided into four scenic areas: the Middle Area, the East Area, the West Area and the North Area, interconnected by a 700-m long zigzag corridor. Both sides of the long corridor are adorned with over 300 sq. m of stone carvings featuring calligraphy from many dynasties, and are known as the Orthodox Calligraphy Models of the Lingering Garden.

Admission:
7:30~17:00
¥40 (Apr.16~Oct.30), ¥30 (Oct.31~Apr.15)
Tel: 0512-65579466
www.gardenly.com

Garden of Cultivation

yi pu

" A garden earns more fame with a better owner." The Garden of Cultivation is an unusual gem because it remained unchanged despite its various owners. Therefore, even though it is small, the garden is part of the World Heritage list. Three well-known scholars possessed the garden: Yuan Zugeng (1519–1590) of the Ming dynasty, who stepped down from his position in the government at the age of 40 to become a widely respected scholar; Wen Zhenmeng (1574–1638), who served as the prime minister in the late Ming dynasty, enjoyed a high reputation as the great-grandson of Wen Zhengming, a celebrated master painter in China's history; and Jiang Cai, a respected

scholar and minister of Foreign Affairs during the late Ming dynasty, who protested against corruption by exiling himself.

The Fish-feeding Pavilion of this garden is the only example of Ming dynasty architecture to have survived through the years. Ancient colored drawings and floral designs remain intact on the roof beams of the pavilion. Take some time to appreciate these precious rarities.

Admission:
8:00~17:00
¥10
Tel: 0512-67271614

Shanghai
Get Started Here

General Information

Shanghai, the largest city in China, is located at the mouth of the Yangtze River. Its phenomenal economic growth in the last 15 years is the talk of Asia and the entire world. The start of the boom began in 1990, and it seems like the skyline of the city changes every month. In the 1920s and 1930s, Shanghai was known as the Paris of the East, but upheaval and war left the city in disarray. Now Shanghai has regained its luster, luring people from all over the world to visit and invest. Shanghai is a place "where yesterday meets tomorrow."

Environment

The vast majority of Shanghai's land area is flat, apart from a few hills in the southwest corner. Shanghai has a humid subtropical climate and experiences four distinct seasons. The most delightful seasons are spring, although the weather conditions can change quickly, and autumn, which is generally sunny and dry. The average temperature is 1~8°C in January and 23~32°C in July.

Places of Interest

The Bund, located along the bank of the Huangpu River, contains a rich collection of early 20th century architecture.

Pudong, literally meaning east of the River lies across from the Bund, exemplifies the most dramatic changes in modern Shanghai. Ten years

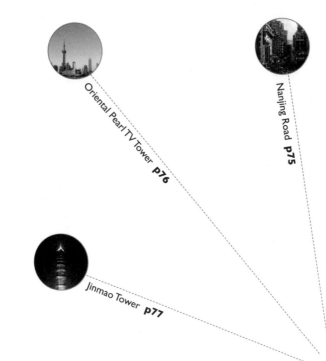

Oriental Pearl TV Tower **p76**

Nanjing Road **p75**

Jinmao Tower **p77**

The Bund and the Huangpu River **p79**

③

Shanghai

Shanghai Museum **p81**

Xintiandi **p83**

Yu Garden **p74**

ago Pudong was mostly rice and vegetable fields, but it has transformed into Shanghai's newest business and residential area, spreading out from Lujiazui, the finance and trade center of the metropolis. The historic classical architecture of the bund and modern skyline of Lujiazui creates an exciting contrast for Shanghai's many visitors.

In Puxi, literally meaning west of the River, the city's historic row home neighborhoods called Shikumen have been refurbished to preserve the essence of Shanghai living during the 1930s. Xintiandi (New Heaven and Earth) located in downtown is the typical successful example. It is a chic area with trendy shops, restaurants and cafes for local fashion lovers and visitors alike.

http://lyw.sh.gov.cn/en/

Shanghai Grand Theater **p85**

Ancient Town of Zhujiajiao **p84**

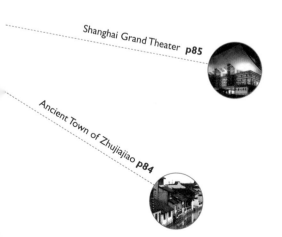

Yu Garden

yu yuan

Admission:
8:30~17:00
¥40 (Apr.1~Jun.30,
Sept.1~Nov.30)
¥30 (The rest months)
Tel: 021-63282465

Yu Garden, a classical garden in downtown Shanghai, dates back over 400 years. Each pavilion, hall, stone and stream in the garden expresses the quintessential South China landscape design from the Ming and Qing dynasties. From over forty spots—divided by dragon walls, wood corridors and beautiful flowers—visitors can take in the garden's many scenes. Strolling in the garden evokes the phrase, "one step, one beauty; every step, every beauty."

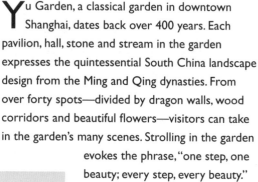

Yu Garden occupies an area of 20,000 sq. m (about 5 ac.). Although the small size does not represent the attractions of the garden, its pavilions, halls, rockeries, ponds and cloisters all have distinctive characteristics. There are six main areas in the garden: Sansui Hall, Wanhua Chamber, Dianchun Hall, Huijing Hall, Yuhua Hall and the Inner Garden. Each area features several scenic spots within its borders.

The surrounding bazaar is packed with traditional and modern shops, restaurants and a temple.

Nanjing Road
nan jing lu

Nanjing Road of Shanghai, known as "China's premier shopping street," stretches around 5.5-mi. from Jing'an Temple in the west to the Bund in the east. The East Nanjing Road pedestrian mall was completed at the 50th anniversary of the People's Republic of China. Huge shopping centers, specialty stores and shops with Chinese specialities line both sides of this street. Shanghai No. 1 Department Store, Hualian Department Store, Shanghai Fashion Co. LTD., and Shanghai No. 1 Foodstuff Store are four major companies that reflect the past and present of Nanjing Road, making it a shopping experience combines traditional and modern styles. West Nanjing Road is known for its luxurious shopping centers, which offer countless famous brands, superior quality, and new fashions. Walking along Nanjing Road, one will find one of the city's most vibrant parts. Flashing neon signs, the fashionable stores flanking the street, the hustling and bustling crowd, the lovely sightseeing trains, the uniquely-designed city sculptures, all reflect the modern urban side of Shanghai.

Oriental Pearl TV Tower
dong fang ming zhu

Admission:
8:30~21:00
¥100 (to the 364-m-high
Sightseeing Hall)
¥150 (to the Three Main
Spheres)
Tel: 021-58791888

The Oriental Pearl Radio and Television Tower is 468 m tall. It has 11 big and small spheres. Besides its height, the tower's impressive architectural design also makes the Oriental Pearl TV Tower an eye-catching feature to the Lujiazui skyline. The entire building is supported by three gigantic columns, which are 9 m in diameter each and start underground. The entire structure rests on rich green grassland and gives the appearance of pearls shining on a jade plate. Together with the Nanpu Bridge and Yangpu Bridge on the Huangpu River, it looks like two dragons playing with a ball.

The various spheres and columns actually house places of interest, commerce, and recreation. Shanghai Urban Historical Development Gallery is on the first floor. The large lower sphere has a futuristic space city and a fabulous sightseeing hall. The pearl at the very top of the tower contains shops, restaurants, including a rotating restaurant, and a sightseeing floor. At nighttime, the tower becomes a brilliant three-dimensional sight, which amazes every visitor.

Jinmao Tower

jin mao da sha

Standing in the Lujiazui financial and business district the Jinmao Tower faces the Bund across from the Huangpu River. With a total height of 420.5 m and 88 floors above ground, the Jinmao Tower—generally regarded as a landmark building of Shanghai—combines elements of Chinese culture with the latest in architectural design.

The observation deck on the 88th floor at 340.1 m covers an area of 1,520 sq. m. The glass wall offers panoramic views all over the city and a magnificent vista of the Yangtze River's estuary.

Admission:
8:30~21:00
¥70
Tel: 021-50475101

This is one of the tallest atriums in the world—a barrel-vaulted atrium, starting from the 56th floor to the 87th. The two express elevators escalate at 9.1 m per second, sending tourists to the top of the building in only 45 seconds.

The Bund and the Huangpu River

wai tan, huang pu jiang

The Bund shows off Shanghai's outstanding buildings that line the Huangpu River of different architectural styles, including Gothic, Baroque, Romanesque, Classicism and the Renaissance. It stretches one mile along the bank of the Huangpu River. Traditionally, the Bund begins at Yan'an Road in the south and ends at Waibaidu Bridge in the north, while crossing over the Suzhou Creek. This row of 52 structures—known as a museum of "buildings in multinational styles of architecture" for combining the Oriental and Occidental—has been regarded as an important landmark in Shanghai for over a century. At

night, floodlights illuminate the attention to detail in each building's design. Nowadays, the Bund is one of the most trendy places in Shanghai, featuring world-class luxury brands. It's a favorite haunt for fashion lovers and the affluent.

The Huangpu River, the largest river and the most important shipping artery of Shanghai, twists and turns like an undulating muddy dragon from the mouth of the Yangtze River to the East China Sea. The yellow and ice-free Huangpu River is 114 km (71 mi.) long, 400 m (0.25 mi.) wide and has an average depth of 9 m (30 ft). The river divides the city into two parts: Puxi (west) and Pudong (east). Whether it is during the day or at night, the views along the river are beautiful. The great modern skyscrapers of Pudong and the classical buildings in different architectural styles in Puxi are records of development during various historical periods. The Huangpu River is a witness for it all.

Shanghai Museum
shang hai bo wu guan

Located on the southern grounds of People's Square, the Shanghai Museum is one of the four major museums in China, garnering the same fame as the Palace Museum, Nanjing Museum, and Xi'an Museum. The museum building with a round top and square base is shaped like an ancient bronze tripod cooking vessel called a *ding*, symbolizing the ancient Chinese perception of the world as a "round sky, square earth."

It has an exhibition area of 12,000 sq. m on four floors. The first floor features the Ancient Chinese Bronze and the Ancient Chinese Sculpture galleries; the second floor has the Ancient Chinese Ceramics gallery; the third floor contains the Chinese Calligraphy, Chinese Painting, and Chinese Seal galleries, and the fourth floor features the Ancient Chinese Jade, Chinese Coin, Chinese Ming and Qing Furniture, Chinese Minority Nationalities' Art galleries. Currently, the museum has a collection of 120 thousand pieces of precious and rare works of art, including bronze, ceramics, calligraphy, furniture, jades, ancient coins, paintings, seals, sculptures, minority art and foreign art, which narrate China's 5,000-year civilization.

Admission:
9:00~17:00 All Year Round
(Entry stops at 16:00)
Ticket Free, Admission Fee
for Special Exhibitions: ¥20
Tel: 021-96968686
www.shanghaimuseum.net

Xintiandi
xin tian di

Located in downtown Shanghai, Xintiandi is a fashionable entertainment pedestrian zone that reflects the city's historical and cultural legacies. This urban complex brings together modern buildings with *shikumen* homes, the main residential homes for Shanghai residents in the early 1900s. It covers an area of 30,000 sq. m. The old *shikumen* underwent restoration to integrate with the new buildings around. The results are preserved *shikumen* exteriors with interiors that embody a different world of international galleries, bars, cafes, boutiques, and theme restaurants, which combine history, culture, tourism, business, entertainment, and residences. The contrast and integration of the past and the present, and of the East and West give Xintiandi an endless charm. It has been an ideal place for foreign and domestic tourists to have a general view of the history, culture, and modern lifestyle of Shanghai, and the best place for people of refined taste to meet and enjoy city life.

Ancient Town of Zhujiajiao

zhu jia jiao

Zhujiajiao is an ancient town located in a suburb of Shanghai at the bank of Dianshan Lake. The town, with a history of over 1,000 years, is the most well preserved ancient town in Shanghai and has been known as the "Venice of Shanghai" In 1991, it was designated by the State Council of China as a "Well-Known Chinese Cultural Town."

Admission:
8:00~16:00
¥80 (for 9 Scenic Spots, including Touring Boat)
¥60 (for 8 Scenic Spots)
¥30 (for 4 Scenic Spots)
Tel: 021-59240077

It has a simple, but attractive appearance typical of towns in southern China. People who live amidst the hustle and bustle of modern city life can find antiquity, lersure and tranquility among the old stone bridges crossing the bubbling streams, small dark-awning boats, weeping willows swaying along the riverbanks, and Ming and Qing styled residences with inviting couryards.

Walking along the zigzagged narrow streets and lanes lined with shops and stores, tourists feel like they're strolling through a simple, but lively wash painting. Exquisite in structure and beautiful in shape, Fangsheng Bridge is the first of the ten attractions in Zhujiajiao. Constructed in the reign of Emperor Wanli of the Ming dynasty, it is the largest joint five-arch stone bridge in Shanghai.

Shanghai Grand Theater

shang hai da ju yuan

The Shanghai Grand Theater is located on the west side of People's Square, next to the Shanghai Municipal Building in the East.

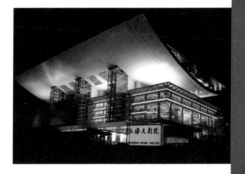

Designed by well-known French architect Jean Marie Charpentier, it combines the Eastern and Western elements in concise and graceful geometrical forms, such as the crown-like white arc-shaped roof bending upwards. It looks like a modern-day crystal palace in the light at night. With its forward style and beautiful outlook, the theater has become a representative building in Shanghai.

On the top of the building, there are outdoor theaters and a mid-air garden that is in the shape of a treasure bowl. The Grand Theater is made up of three parts with a total floor space of 70,000 sq. m. The lyric theater for ballet, musical and symphony performances has 1,800 seats divided into the auditorium, the 2nd and the 3rd-floors, and six balconies. The drama theater has 750 seats and the studio theater has 300 seats. Moreover, the Shanghai Grand Theater also has 12 rehearsal halls, gymnasiums, scene-setting rooms, make-up rooms, banquet halls, cultural exhibition halls, and underground garages.

Stop 4: Hangzhou ④

Get Started Here

General Information

Hangzhou, one of the seven ancient capitals and a scenic tourism and historic cultural city in China, was once praised as "the most splendid and luxurious city in the world" by Marco Polo, the Italian traveler in the 13th century. Now it's the provincial capital of Zhejiang Province in southeast China.

Environment

Hangzhou is located in the southern part of the Yangtze River Delta, at the western end of Hangzhou Bay, in the lower reaches of the Qiantang River, and at the southern terminus of the Beijing-Hangzhou Grand Canal. Under the subtropical and monsoon conditions, Hangzhou has four distinct seasons with a mild and humid climate and plenty of sunshine and rainfall. The average temperature is 16.2℃ round year, 28.6℃ in the summer and 3.8℃ in the winter. The average annual rainfall is 1,435 mm and the average relative humidity is 76%.

Places of Interest

As a key national tourist destination, and historic cultural city named by the State Council of China, Hangzhou is renowned as a "Paradise on Earth," "Cultural State," "Home to Silk," "Home of Tea" and "Land of Fish and Rice." Some museums reflecting this diverse culture can be found in Hangzhou.

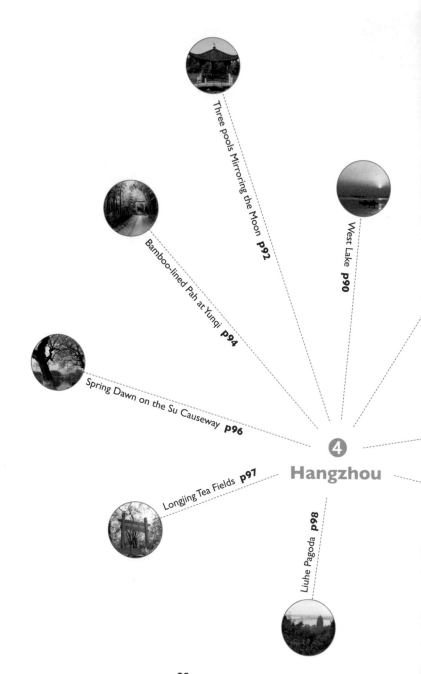

Three pools Mirroring the Moon **p92**

West Lake **p90**

Bamboo-lined Pah at Yunqi **p94**

Spring Dawn on the Su Causeway **p96**

Longjing Tea Fields **p97**

④

Hangzhou

Liuhe Pagoda **p98**

Lingyin Monastery **p101**

West Lake is undoubtedly the most renowned feature of Hangzhou. There are numerous historical sites and stunning vistas around West Lake. The "Ten West Lake Prospects" have been especially selected to give a visitor outstanding views of the lake, mountains and monuments.

www.gotohz.com

Peak Flown from Afar **p100**

General Yue's Temple and Tomb **p99**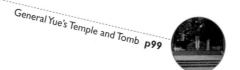

West Lake

xi hu

Hangzhou and its West Lake have been immortalized by countless poets and artists. The west lake was called Golden Cow Lake before the Song dynasty because a golden cow was said to materialize on its waters whenever a sage or holy man passed by. Later, the poet Su Shi (Dongpo) (1037–1101) compared the lake with the famous beauty Xi Shi, writing that like the courtesan, "it is attractive with make-up or without." The lake site used to be a shallow bay connected to the Hangzhou Bay but was gradually sealed off by alluvial deposit, and dredging and landscaping did the rest.

This oval-shaped lake has an area of about 2.3 sq. mi. (6 sq. km) and a circumference of 9.3 mi. (15 km). The average depth of the lake is about 5 ft (1.5 m), with the deepest part being only 9 ft (2.8 m) and the shallowest spot less than 3.3 ft (1 m).

The city of Hangzhou stands on its eastern shore. On the gentle slopes of the hills surrounding the three sides of the lake are large gardens displaying a variety of flora: peach blossom in spring, lily in summer, osmanthus in autumn and plum blossom in winter. The hills are dotted with pavilions, pagodas, grottoes, mansions and streams.

The lake also adds its beauty and mystique to the Ten Beautiful Sites of Hangzhou—Autumn Moon over the Smooth Lake, Spring Dawn on the Su Causeway, Snow over the Broken Bridge, Dusk at the Thunder Peak Pagoda, Evening Bell from Nanping, Waving Lotuses on a Garden Pond, Golden Carp in Huagang, Listening to the Nightingales under Willows on Lakeside, Three Pools Mirroring the Moon and Double Peaks Piercing the Clouds.

Three Pools Mirroring the Moon

san tan ying yue

Three Pools Mirroring the Moon is the largest and finest artificial isle in West Lake. It is also called the Lesser Yingzhou Isle after a legendary islet in the depths of the Eastern China Sea. The islet covers 7 hectare including the water surface and the area called "a lake within an island and an island within a lake." Three small gourd-shaped pagodas were built afterwards in the south lake of the islet, which is the origin of the name "three pools." A general named Peng Yulin, after retiring from his official post, built for himself a garden villa on the island at the beginning of the Qing dynasty. Zigzag bridges and pavilions were later

additions. Three Pools Mirroring the Moon today is the result of a large scale refurbishing project around the end of the Qing dynasty.

The three stone miniature pagodas standing in the lake off the isle are presumably the best place for moon viewing. On the night of the Mid-Autumn Festival, the isle and its three miniature pagodas are a prime attraction for moon spectators. Lights are put inside the windows of the pagoda. The water near the pagoda reflects the shiny lights and the moon. The moon in the sky, water, and hearts of onlookers further accentuates the beauty of this scenic spot.

Admission:
8:00~17:00
¥20
Tel: 0571-87065684

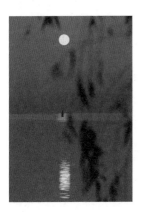

Bamboo-lined Path at Yunqi

yun qi zhu jing

This attraction is located southwest of West Lake on the North Bank of the Qiantang River and in the Wuyun Hill Yunqi Village. "Yunqi" means clouds lingering. The Bamboo-lined Path at Yunqi is well-known for its quietness and coolness. Among the trees around the path, one of the Chinese sweet gum tree is over a 1000 years old. Hundreds of thousands of bamboo surround the famous stone-paved footpath leading into the Yunqi valley. Walking along, the Mind Purifying Pond, which means "a pure mind," appears on the path. The cool and clear water, refreshing sounds of nature, and picturesque environment make it a relaxing place for people from the city.

Three ages-old pavilions were constructed to complete the bamboo-lined path: "Mind Purifying Pavilion," "Dragon Back Pavilion" and "Meeting-Rain Pavilion." It's a wonderful experience to enjoy the rain while listening to the sound of raindrops beating on the leaves sitting in the pavilion.

In each season, different scenes delight visitors. In spring, shoots grow among the forest; in summer, the cool breeze carries the fragrance of the trees; in autumn, the forest over the surrounding hills turns color; and in winter, the whole valley is cloaked in white.

Admission:
7:00~18:00
¥8
Tel: 0571-87090437

Spring Dawn on the Su Causeway

su di chun xiao

The three km-long Su Causeway became a tourist attraction as early as 1090. It is named after the famous personality who constructed it—Northern Song dynasty poet Su Dongpo, who organized a large scale dredging of the lake and then created causeway with the silt from the dredging during his term as the city's governor. Today's causeway is the result of many refurbishing projects over the centuries.

The causeway consists of six single-span stone arch bridge that offer different views: Yingbo (reflecting the waves), Suolan (locking the waves), Wangshan (looking at distant hills), Yadi (causeway ballast), Dongpu (eastern ford), and Kuahong (spanning rainbow). The embankments along the way are lined with graceful willows and various flowers. Visitors can stand on the causeway and view the lake far and near through the willow branches. In the evening, the causeway is illuminated by lights, making it a romantic spot for promenading couples. In spring, the scenery of Su Causeway is the most enchanting, giving it the specific name "Spring Dawn on the Su Causeway."

Admission:
Ticket free
Tel: 0571-87025793

Longjing Tea Fields
long jing cha yuan

Longjing (Dragon Well) Tea is one of the most renowned Chinese green teas. Its name comes from where the best quality tea of this kind is cultivated. The village is right outside Hangzhou. The tea's history and the village are full of legend with the royal family of the Qing dynasty.

The best time for visiting Longjing Tea Fields is during the harvest period, usually from the first week of March until after early May. Farm hands pick the fresh tea leaves throughout the fields. This spring harvest is the best quality to purchase because tea crops later on in the year have had their leaves damaged by rain.

Admission:
8:00~17:00
¥35
Tel: 0571-86086364

Liuhe Pagoda
liu he ta

The Liuhe Pagoda, also known as Six Harmonies Pagoda, stands on the Qiantang River in Hangzhou and was first erected in AD 970 in the belief that it would help placate mischievous spirits and control local flooding. The present brick pagoda was built in 1533, and its wooden eaves were renovated in 1899. The octagonal pagoda is nearly 200 ft (60 m) high, with 104 iron wind bells playing from the corners of its eaves.

Admission:
6:00~18:30
¥20 (¥10 for the Pagoda)
Tel: 0517-86591401

General Yue's Temple and Tomb

yue wang miao

Two rows of red-lacquered pillars lead to the main hall of the Temple of General Yue (1103–1142), each engraved with scenes of his most famous Song dynasty battles against Jin invaders. Another engraving displays the characters *xin zhao tian ri* (Heart as Clear as Sun in Sky), based on the general's last words before execution. The seated statue of the great warrior was only recently cast and installed. Over it hangs a plaque inscribed with four Chinese characters *huan wo he shan* (Restore to Us Our Land and Rivers), and the ceiling is painted with more than 370 white cranes, symbolizing loftiness and staunch loyalty.

Admission:
7:30~17:00
¥25
Tel: 0571-87960089

Peak Flown from Afar
fei lai feng

飛來峰

There are as many as 300 stone carvings that adorn the walls and cave of Peak Flown from Afar near the Lingyin Monastery. The most well-known sculpture is that of Maitreya in the form of the Laughing Buddha. Its name comes from the monastery's founder, the Indian monk Huili, who is said to have commented on a visit there: "This looks a hill of the Immortal Vulture Mountain of Tianzhu. I wonder when it flew and settled here." The sculptures shown here were begun in the Five dynasties (AD 907–AD 960) and added to in the reigns of the Song and Yuan.

Admission:
6:00~18:30
¥35
Tel: 0571-87969691

Lingyin Monastery

ling yin si

This famous monastery stands to the northwest of West Lake in Hangzhou. Its site was selected in AD 326 (Eastern Jin dynasty) by the Indian abbot Huili, who decided it was a fitting "hermitage for the Immortals." During the Five dynasties following the collapse of Han rule, the devoutly Buddhist Zian Liu, the prince of Yue, greatly expanded the monastery to include nine mansions, 18 pavilions and 3000 monks and novices. When the Qing emperor Kangxi visited the huge complex on his trip to southern China, he gave it the name Cloud Forest Zen Monastery (Yunlin Chansi). The monastery still features its ornate Great Hall, a 110-ft (33.6-m) high structure that houses a 30-ft (9.1-m) tall gilded statue of Sakyamuni Buddha sitting on a lotus pedestal, based on a well-known sculpture of the Tang dynasty. A lengthy couplet describing famous scenic spots in Hangzhou is inscribed on two tall pillars in front of the statue. The hall is also decked with other images and paintings representing Buddhist mythology, and two ancient stone plaques with inscriptions from the scriptures.

Admission:
6:00~18:30
¥30
Tel: 0571-87987019

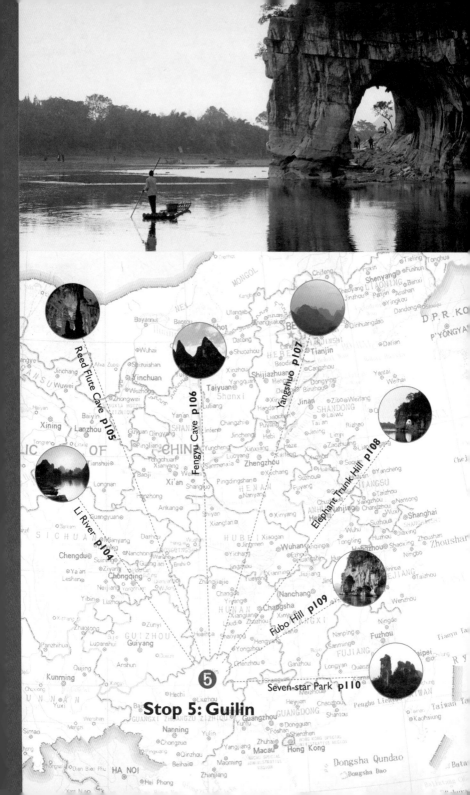

Reed Flute Cave p105

Fengyu Cave p106

Yangshuo p107

Elephant Trunk Hill p108

Li River p104

Fubo Hill p109

Seven-star Park p110

Stop 5: Guilin

Get Started Here

General Information

Situated in the northeastern part of Guangxi Zhuang Autonomous Region on the west bank of the Li River, Guilin has long enjoyed the reputation for the most fantastic natural landscapes in China. It was named after the fragrance of the osmanthus tree. As a popular Chinese saying goes, "Guilin's scenery is best among all under heaven." Its natural wonders—magical green pinnacles, crystal-clear water, picturesque rocks and intriguing caves—provide a fascinating and exciting travel experience.

Environment

Covering an area of about 4,195 sq. km, the city's municipal region is rather compact compared with other leading Chinese cities. It lies in a basin surrounded by the Yuecheng Range, Ocean Hill, Jiaqiao Range and Tianping Hill. The altitude is 140 to 160 m. The climate of Guilin is warm, moist, and moderate year round with an annual precipitation of about 1900 mm. The average temperature year round is 19℃. The coldest temperature occurs in January at 8℃ and the hottest occurs in July at 28℃ . The best time to travel here is between April and October.

Places of Interest

The Two-River and Four-Lake Water System coils the small city, which recreates the flourishing scenery of the Song dynasty. There are many complete karsts, large soaring limestone structures, which form part of the captivating landscape in this area. The primary attractions can be summed up as "Three hills, Two caves and One river" referring to Diecai, Fubo and Elephant Trunk hills, Reed Flute and Seven-Star caves, and the world-renowned Li River. Nearby the river is a Stone Museum that displays intriguing geological finds.

www.guilintourist.com

Li River

li jiang

Fishermen on bamboo rafts, their lamps lit to attract shoals of fish, add to the fairyland effect of the Li River and its most scenic stretch between Guilin and Yangshuo. The men use tamed cormorants to make their catches. The Li River, a principal tributary of the River Gwei, flows from Xing'an northwest of Guilin through to Yangshuo and then joins the West River after a distance of 272 mi. (437 km).

Its waters are varied. The Guilin-Yangshuo stretch is so placid that one can see the pebbles lying on the riverbed. Elsewhere, the rapids can be difficult to negotiate.

The numerous, rugged peaks on the two sides of the meandering river offer a feast to the river traveler's eye. Yuan Mei (1716–1798), the Qing poet, marveled at the swift-changing scenery and made the following observation of the river tour. "One moment, you see the green peaks floating over your head; the next they glide under your boat."

Reed Flute Cave
lu di yan

This magnificent cavern, packed with bizarre rock formations and stalactites and stalagmites, is in the slope of Guangming Mountain, 4 mi. (6 km) northwest of Guilin City. It was first discovered in antiquity, and inscriptions have been found on its walls dating back at least 1000 years. But somehow, probably because of civil war, it was forgotten for some time and then rediscovered—some say the local people kept it a secret, using it as a convenient hiding place in times of war.

Reed Flute Cave measures 787 ft (240 m) across and is divided into two sections separated by a pond forming a natural barrier. The cave features a rock called the Old Scholar, named after a sage who is said to have been so enchanted by Guilin's scenery that he began a poem about it— but, unable to conjure up words adequate enough to finish it, he turned to stone.

Other rock formations take the shape of a horse, a lion, a drum or a zither—all uncannily true to life. The cave is illuminated, and visitors are able to take in an enjoyable tour that covers about 1641 ft (500 m).

Admission:
7:30~18:00 (Apr. 1~Oct. 30),
8:00~17:30 (Nov. 1~Mar. 30)
¥60
Tel: 0773-2695075

Fengyu Cave

feng yu yan

Admission:
8:30~17:30
¥60
Tel: 0773-7128569
www.cnfyy.cn

Located in Shanhe 68 mi. (110 km) southeast of Guilin, Fengyu Cave is a 3.3 mi. (5.3 km) long karst cave with a subterranean river 1.4 mi. (2.3 km) long. It is named after a kind of red fish in the cave river, called Feng Yu. The cave passes 9 karst peaks and has with many large chambers, the biggest of which is more than 274,480 sq. ft (25,000 sq. m).

First developed in 1994, Fengyu Cave has been a popular and revered showpiece of the Guilin area. The stalagmites in Fengyu Cave are fairly young and are growing quickly. Most of them are slender and some paper thin. One typical stalagmite, named Ding Hai Shen Zhen (Marvelous Needle) is 32 ft (9.8 m) high but only about 5.9 in. (15 cm) in diameter. The cave can be visited by a 30-minute walk through different rock formations, followed by a boat tour on the underground river.

Yangshuo

yang shuo

There is a well-known saying that goes, "The rivers and hills of Guilin are the most beautiful in China, and those of Yangshuo surpass Guilin's."

Certainly, the contrast of limestone and tropical green, and the hills and their surrounding flat paddy lands, is one scenic aspect of this karst landscape. The Li River winds through the hills like a green silk ribbon. The town of Yangshuo itself, at the end of a 50-mi. (80-km) boat cruise from Guilin City, is one of the most picturesque centers of the area and is surrounded by karst peaks that resemble ancient Chinese hats, galloping horses, a paintbrush and a five-fingered hand. All this, packed into a small town area, has inspired the following Tang dynasty saying: "The town walls encircle less than two *li* of space, but all the houses are hidden among ten thousand hills."

To the north of Yangshuo lies Xingping, which is reputed to have "the best of Yangshuo's landscape." There, fishing rafts crisscrossing the Li River against a dramatic backdrop of hills are a typical sight.

Admission:
Tel: 0773-8827922

Elephant Trunk Hill
xiang bi shan

Admission:
6:30~22:00 (Apr.1~Oct.30),
7:00~21:30 (Nov.1~Mar.30)
¥25
Tel: 0773-2803000

This is another imaginatively shaped outcrop at the confluence of Guilin's Yang and Li Rivers, and the subject of a sad legend. It is said that the King of Heaven, taking a tour of southern China, brought with him an elephant that fell ill in Guilin. A local farmer nursed it back to health, and the elephant worked for him in the fields in return. The Heavenly King considered this a betrayal and put the poor creature to death. It promptly turned to stone.

Fubo Hill
fu bo shan

Standing solitarily by the Li River in downtown Guilin, Fubo Hill is an impressive karst structure, surrounded by rolling green hills and waters, caves, picturesque rocks, and gardens. A climb to the top of the hill offers visitors an extensive view of charming scenery.

Some believe the name comes from the rock formation's interruption of the Li River's flow. As one of Guilin's enchanting attractions, Fubo Hill's caves contain well-preserved Buddhist paintings, drawings and calligraphy dating back to the Tang dynasty. The Returned Pearl Cave (Huan Zhu Dong) and Thousand Buddha Cave (Qian Fo Yan) are two of the best for ancient artwork. One stalactite in the Returned Pearl Cave, known as the Sword-Testing Stone is worthy of mention. It nearly hangs to the ground and is said to be the place General Fubo tested his sword.

Admission:
6:30~18:30 (Apr.1~Oct.30),
7:00~18:30 (Nov.1~Mar.30)
¥15
Tel: 0773-2800318

Seven-star Park
qi xing gong yuan

This park was part of the first batch of National Tour Attractions officially recognized by the China National Tourism Administration. It is also the largest and most comprehensive park in Guilin with an area of 134.7 hectare. With its long history and numerous attractions, such as Camel Hill, Natural Stone Hall, Seven-star Cave, and Crescent Pavilion, it has been a tourist highlight since the Sui (AD 581–AD 618) and Tang dynasties.

Camel Hill
(骆驼峰 *luo tuo feng*)

Camel Hill looks so remarkably like a camel that it is difficult to imagine calling it by another name. However,

there is another name that has
a story to go along with it. The
hill is sometimes called Ewer Hill
because it is also shaped like a
wine ewer. At its foot, there is a
spot called the Grave of Lei the
Drinker—commemorating Lei
Mingchun of the Ming dynasty

who used to climb to the summit to drown his
sorrows in wine, lamenting the collapse of the Ming.

Flower Bridge
(花桥 *hua qiao*)

Inside the park, the renowned flower Bridge is a
must-see. This elegant bridge, built of rock, reflects
traditional Han Chinese architecture. It was rebuilt
in 1540 during the Ming rule at the confluence of
the Small East River and Lingjian River in Guilin.
It is 410 ft (125 m) long, with a total of 11 arches
across its entire length. A green-tiled roof provides
"wind-rain" protection, but is not as dramatic as
the style of the Dong ethnic minority group. To the
east of the bridge stands Hibiscus Rock. The name
sounds pretty, but it is actually a symbol of suffering.
It bears the watermarks of many floods that have
swept across the area in the past.

Admission:
6:00~20:30
¥65
Tel: 0773-5814342

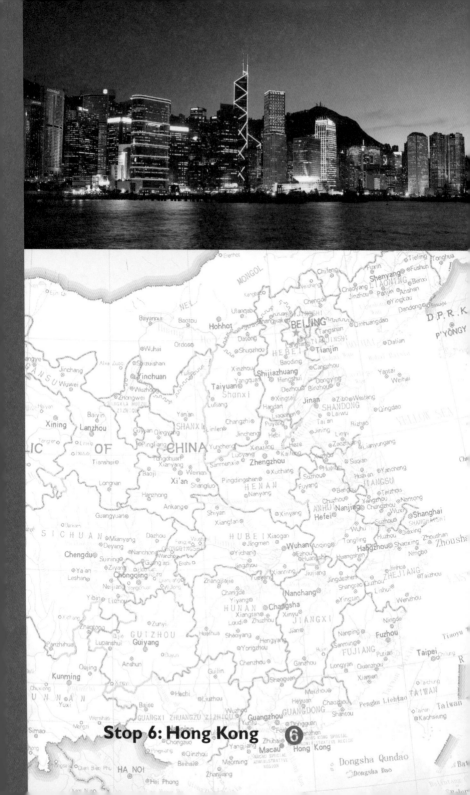

Stop 6: Hong Kong ⑥

Get Started Here

General Information

Situated at the southern tip of China, Hong Kong is ideally positioned at the center of rapidly developing East Asia. Described as a "barren rock" over 150 years ago, it has become an excellent financial, trading and business center and, a premier world city. Hong Kong's population was about 6.94 million in mid-2005. It is one of the most densely populated areas in the world. Hong Kong has large amount of foreign expatriates, making up about 5 percent of the total population. The top three nationalities come from the Philippines, Indonesia, and Thailand.

Environment

With a total area of 1,104 sq. km, it covers Hong Kong Island, Kowloon Peninsula just opposite of the island, and the New Territories —the more rural section of Hong Kong, which also includes 262 outlying islands. Hong Kong is an year round destination with a mild weather from the middle of September to the end of February, and a warm and humid climate for the rest of the year. About 90 percent of the rainfall occurs between April and September.

Places of Interest

There are several important attractions to catch for first-time visitors. A voyage on the fabled Star Ferry, the Peak Tram, the islands, Po Lin Monastery, Lan Kwai Fong and Repulse Bay showcase Hong Kong's

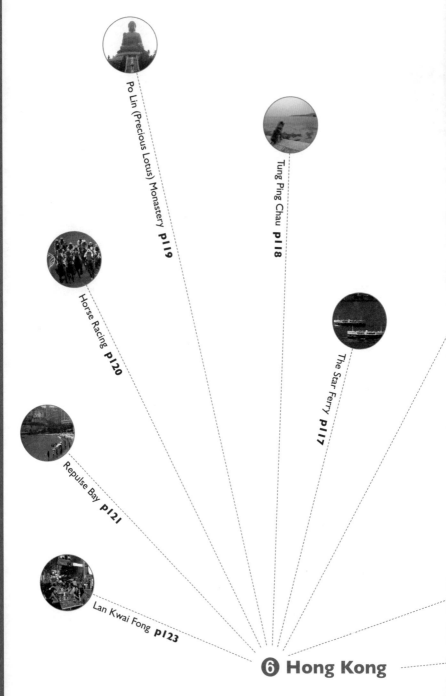

Po Lin (Precious Lotus) Monastery **P119**

Tung Ping Chau **p118**

Horse Racing **P120**

The Star Ferry **P117**

Repulse Bay **p121**

Lan Kwai Fong **p123**

❻ Hong Kong

Hong Kong Electric Tram **p116**

unique culture that combines Eastern and Western influences.

The cuisine of Hong Kong reflects these influences. More great restaurants are here than any place on earth. They serve the national dishes of two-dozen different countries, as well as the cuisine of virtually every province in China. The reason for the superb food in Hong Kong is simple: the Cantonese are natural gourmets. The topic of food is fundamental to the people of Hong Kong. No wonder that it is called the gourmet paradise of Asia.

Hong Kong is a shopper's delight, with a vast selection of merchandise available. It is said that anything made in the world can be found here.

www.discoverhongkong.com

Ocean Park **p126**

The Peak **p124**

Hong Kong Electric Tram

xiang gang dian che

www.hktramways.com

The HK Tramways is one of the oldest public transportation systems still in operation. Inaugurated in 1904, 16 years after the Peak Tram started its service in 1888, it has provided the public with the cheapest way to travel across Hong Kong Island from Kennedy Town to Sau Kei Wan, with a branch serving the Happy Valley Racecourse. Its slow ride offers travelers a safe and leisurely way to have a first-hand look at local street life and the town. There are even open-balcony trams for tourists and private hire. While most of the trams are old-styled with slide windows, new modern trams in green and white were added to the fleet in 2000, which are more comfortable than the old ones.

The Star Ferry

tian xing xiao lun

The Star Ferry's green-and-white boats are the oldest in the network of Hong Kong ferries. Founded in 1898, it has served as a major communication route between Hong Kong Island and Kowloon. Lovingly cared for, they also cover the shortest distance between the Central business area and the busy shopping area in Tsimshatui. While it is still commonly used as an inexpensive mode of transportation, the 10-minute Star Ferry ride offers panoramic views of the Victoria Harbor, with IFC Phase II, the Bank of China and Hong Kong and Shanghai Bank buildings and Central Plaza on the Hong Kong side, and the HK Cultural Center, the Peninsula Hotel and Regent Hotel on the Kowloon side.

www.starferry.com.hk

Tung Ping Chau
dong ping zhou

A visit to Tung Ping Chau provides a glimpse of Hong Kong that combines colorful history and remote island isolation. A tiny island in the New Territories that has been turned into a marine park, Tung Ping Chau was used long ago by smugglers to bring guns and opium from hinterland. Almost deserted today, the main village on the island still has a few families, who offer services to weekend vacationers. A hike through the pleasant parklands is a good place to spot wild orchids native to the Hong Kong area. The island's footpaths will eventually lead to each end of the island, where there are large rock outcrops. At the island's south end are two huge rocks called Drum Rock or Watchman's Tower Rock. The long thick rock is part of the layer of rock that resembles a dragon's back. At its northern end, it is called Lung Luk Shui or "dragon entering the water."

Po Lin (Precious Lotus) Monastery

bao lian si

Visitors who want to explore the outer islands in Hong Kong often make the trip to Po Lin Monastery on Hong Kong's largest island, Lautau. When first built by three monks in 1906, it only had a shrine dedicated to Buddha. It was given the current name "Po Lin Monastery" in 1924, and was expanded over the years to become one of the top ten Buddhist monasteries in Hong Kong. The world's largest bronze Buddha, 100 ft (30 m) tall and weighing 275 tons, sits on the top of Muyu (wood fish) Peak across the monastery, truly an impressive sight for all who hike up the peak to the statue.

Admission:
9:00~18:00 (Monastery)
10:00~18:00 (Big Buddha)
Vegetarian Meals Serving
Hours: 11:30~17:00
Tel: 0852-29855248

Horse Racing
sai ma

Hong Kong has a long horse racing tradition. Horse racing is the most popular spectator sports in this city, which has one of the biggest jockey clubs in the world. With perfect racing courses, Hong Kong was designated as the venue of the 2008 Olympic equestrian events.

Hong Kong's famous racetracks are worth a stop. The 150-year-old Happy Valley Racecourse on Hong Kong Island and the striking Sha Tin Racecourse in the New Territories, just north of the Kowloon peninsula, can be reached via a comfortable air-conditioned train from the Central District. You will not experience horse racing like this anywhere else in the world. The racing season runs from September until June.

www.hkjc.com

Repulse Bay
qian shui wan

Sun-drenched Repulse Bay, located in the south part of Hong Kong Island, is one of the most popular beaches in Hong Kong. Its name comes from a battle where the British fleet repulsed pirates who occupied the beach as a base.

It is always packed with local swimmers and visitors in the summer. Besides aquatic activities, Repulse Bay is a luxurious residential area for dining and relaxation that provides extensive facilities. There are restaurants and barbeque sites at the back of the beach. In addition, the area is dotted with hotels, supermarkets, and cafes.

The Zhenhai Tower Park, built in the traditional Chinese style, is located near the beach. Towering twin

statues of Kwun Yum and Tin Hau, both protectors of fishermen, sit in front of the park. Overlooking Repulse Bay, is the famous "building with a hole."

The clear sparkling water with temperatures ranging from 16 °C to 26 °C year round, and the soft and golden sands lure visitors to Repulse Bay. In addition to these, "The Repulse Bay" and "The Repulse Bay Center" are the landmarks of Repulse Bay. "The Repulse Bay" is a residential apartment that was built on a former hotel site. "The Repulse Bay Center" in front of it is a very elegant and beautiful European building. It has a few restaurants and shops, and was filmed in a popular Hong Kong movie as well. This is certainly another place to go besides the beach.

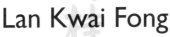

Lan Kwai Fong

lan gui fang

Lan Kwai Fong is Hong Kong's popular haunt for dining, drinking and entertainment. This district is filled with over 100 trendy and stylish restaurants, offering a range of foods from Indian and Russian to Japanese and Californian. The street Lan Kwai Fong is L-shaped and joins with D'Aguilar Street. Both streets turn 90 degrees to form a rectangle. The gleaming atmosphere also spreads throughout the surrounding neighborhoods.

Just around the corner from the city's busy Central business district, it's the perfect place for after-work drinks and dinner with friends. When it comes to nightlife, venture down Lan Kwai Fong to find yourself in the center of the city's hottest nightspots. It's fun to stroll the streets during the evenings to see the true international mix of Hong Kong's cultural cocktail.

www.lankwaifong.com

The Peak
tai ping shan ding

As the highest mountain at 522 m above sea level on Hong Kong Island, the Peak was the exclusive residential area for expatriates before 1947. The more privileged early residents made it the perfect retreat from Hong Kong's summer.

Until 1881, Alexander Findlay Smith, who had worked for Scotland's Highland Railway, managed to petition the Governor for tram routes connecting the south of Murray Barracks to Victoria Gap on the Peak. From then on, the peak gained further development.

Nowadays, a regular and reliable public transportation peak tram is available. More than a century old, this funicular tram travels up the mountain by huge steel cables,

and near the top it reaches a white-knuckle pitch of 45 degrees before leveling off at 1,600 ft. The Peak offers spectacular views of the city and the harbor. It attracts some seven million visitors a year, making it one of Hong Kong's top tourist destinations.

Make sure to catch the best time—an hour before dusk to have ample time to stroll around the summit before watching a hundred million city lights start to twinkle in the city below.

www.thepeak.com.hk

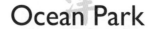

Ocean Park
hai yang gong yuan

As the city's most acclaimed amusement park, Ocean Park covers more than 870,000 sq. m of land on the southern side of Hong Kong Island. Over 4 million people visit the Ocean Park each year. The park's popularity earned it a spot on Forbes top ten theme park list.

The different parts of the park are connected by a 1.5-km long cable car system, as well as the world's second longest outdoor escalator. The journey walking around the park also offers breathtaking panoramic views of the southern side of Hong Kong and the South China Sea.

At the headland, the Park boasts some of its most

exciting rides overlooking the sea, including the Dragon, Abyss Turbo Drop, Crazy Galleon, Ferris Wheel, Ocean Park Tower, and Flying Swing. At the lowland, visitors can experience the joy and thrill of a ride on a 22 m diameter helium balloon that will soar 100 m into the air in the Sky Fair.

Admission:
10:00~18:00
HK$208/Adult, HK$103/
Child (3~11)
Tel: 0852-25520291
www.oceanpark.com.hk